BREAKING

THE

CYCLE

THE ULTIMATE SOLUTION
to DESTRUCTIVE PATTERNS

BREAKING

THE

CYCLE

THE ULTIMATE SOLUTION
to DESTRUCTIVE PATTERNS

DR. JAMES B. RICHARDS

BREAKING THE CYCLE: THE ULTIMATE SOLUTION TO DESTRUCTIVE PATTERNS

Published in the United States of America
© 2003 by Dr. James B. Richards

Milestones International Publishers
an Imprint of True Potential Publishers
True Potential Publishing, Inc.
P.O. Box 904
Travelers Rest, SC 29690
http://tppress.com
www.milestonesintl.com
864-836-4111 ext.107

Cover design by: Chris Gilbert, UDG
DesignWorks www.udgdesignworks.com

3 4 5 6 7 8 9 10 11 / 15 14 13 12

DEDICATION

God never gives up on an individual, but sometimes other people do. I thank God for the people who never gave up on me. They believed in me even when no one else did.

I dedicate this book to Dennis Peacock, my brother-in-law, a church member, a trusted friend, and a co-laborer in this message. Your friendship, your belief in me, and your commitment to this message have been a constant encouragement. You have helped me touch millions of lives.

Thank you!

BREAKING THE CYCLE

THE ULTIMATE SOLUTION TO DESTRUCTIVE PATTERNS

For the free companion video series to this book and other special offers please visit:

http://www.truepotentialmedia.com/breaking-the-cycle/

Contents

CHAPTER 1

THE DEFINING MOMENT

I WILL NEVER FORGET THE CHANCE REUNION. It became for me a defining moment in which I decided, *I must find solutions to these types of problems—solutions for myself and for others*. I had not seen Bob for a few years, but at one time his life had been such an inspiration to me. Now he looked different somehow. I couldn't tell what was wrong, but it was as if he had changed in some way. The sparkle was gone from his eyes. His trademark smile that once defined his presence had faded. He just wasn't the man I remembered.

As we chatted, he seemed to avoid eye contact. It grew more uncomfortable by the minute. As the small talk waned to an embarrassing lull, the emptiness I sensed was more than I could bear. "Bob, you've changed. Have you been doing all right?" The question blundered from my lips. After a hesitation that seemed like an eternity, he looked me in the eye for the first time and shockingly replied, "No, Jim, things aren't all right!"

As I recovered my composure and tried to hide my feeling of shock, I finally convinced this old friend to have coffee with me. His reluctance became more understandable as his story unfolded. The next hour was a painful revelation of how Bob had spent the past fifteen years struggling internally before he finally just gave up. His words burned into my mind, searing like a branding iron: "Life seemed easier before I got saved. I haven't been truly happy for years."

*"Life seemed easier before I got saved.
I haven't been truly happy for years."*

What Had Happened?

Bob had made a commitment to follow Jesus years ago. He wanted to experience the promises of God. He wanted a better life. Like most people who begin this journey, he started off great. He read his Bible and began to understand how to live a totally new quality of life. I remember how he talked about finding the answers for which he had searched all his life.

The first few years of his Christian experience were incredible. His marriage problems began to be resolved. He found new inner resources to love his wife. He even found the strength to face many of his internal issues about relationships and intimacy. His business began to grow as he discovered the values of integrity, dependability, and responsibility. Before long he was one of the most successful contractors in our area. Because of his life, many people came to Jesus to find what he had found.

Then Bob moved to another area and left our simple fellowship of "converted hippies." He became a part of a more organized church that had a lot of great programs. It was a very exciting environment that had a lot to offer. He was very active and committed. Then it seemed like he hit some invisible wall that not only stopped him from moving forward in his growth and development, but also caused him to take a nosedive. He vanished from my "radar screen." He stopped writing. He didn't return calls. For several years he virtually disappeared—until he moved back to town and we happened upon one another.

At first Bob expressed shame about his failures. I was amazed. I had never seen him condemn anyone else who had failed. I couldn't imagine where this was coming from. The truth was, his self-loathing had done more damage to him than his actual "sins." It had become a driving force that affected his every decision and emotion.

After we talked a while, he seemed to finish venting. I thought he would be relieved and that we could get down to some recovery. But just the opposite occurred. Once the shame was gone, something else emerged. I sort of felt like I was driving in fog. I couldn't see exactly where I was going, but I had the eerie sense that a collision was just ahead. I was right. Suddenly, like an unsuspecting driver who breaks through the fog into an unexpected traffic jam, Bob hit head on. It was like everything he feared, everything he hated, and everything he dreaded all surfaced at one time. And I was in front of him.

As the minutes passed, it became more than obvious that Bob was mad at the church, not at me. He felt that the church had led him down a path that stole what he once had in Jesus. He didn't know exactly what had happened; he just knew that it all changed when he got involved with the new church.

Bob was like thousands of people I have talked to. He started out great, but somewhere along the line he got off course. Like many believers, he associated his problem with church. He was not sure what the church had done, but he held the church and its people responsible. He started following Jesus to find a better quality of life, and he enjoyed that new life for a period of time. Now he had lost it, and he did not know how. He just knew that he did not feel right about himself—and he hadn't for a long time. When he went for counseling, it seemed to be little more than a list of religious duties he was told he should follow. He even believed that most of the counseling had made him feel worse about himself instead of better.

I promised Bob that life could get a lot better—and quickly. I explained that he had fallen into the cycle of lack. He had replaced Jesus with religion. Although he was partially justified in his frustration with the church world, I explained that until he assumed responsibility for the places where he had surrendered his personal relationship with God, he would not find much relief.

I explained that he had fallen into the cycle of lack. He had replaced Jesus with religion.

It has been great watching Bob find his way back to peace and joy. He has become a missionary in reaching out to those who have lost their passion for life. Like Morpheus in the movie *The Matrix*, he has devoted his life to disconnecting people from the matrix of religion, illusion, and dead works. He lovingly brings them back to the land of reality in Jesus.

In Search of Happiness

Mankind is on a quest for happiness, peace, and fulfillment. This desire is part of our God-given nature. God created us to live in happiness and peace. Whether you believe in God or not, you are looking for the good things in life. Everyone wants a good life! In the heart of every person there is a desperate longing to experience a quality of life beyond what most will ever know. For some that longing is more like a deep, unidentifiable ache or an illusive dream that lingers just beyond our conscious awareness.

This vague sense of lack can drive people to commit every imaginable sin in their pursuit of happiness. It drives others to seek out thrills and adventure. Still others will vainly strive for perfection through religious performance and legalism. It is like a search for mysterious treasure. Every day we are driven on some level to identify and discover this nebulous source of evasive satisfaction.

When people come to Jesus and make Him their Lord and Savior, they are seeking this quality of life. In fact, the Bible promises that following Jesus with our whole heart will result in an incredible quality of life. In Him we have our first real promise of hope. In Him are the answers to all the longings in life. You see, our relationship with God should not be the end of the search, but the beginning of the journey that leads to life at its best. Meeting Jesus should be the best day in our life. But walking with Jesus for the rest of our life should make every day get better and better. Jesus Himself said, *"My purpose is to*

> *Our relationship with God should not be the end of the search, but the beginning of the journey that leads to life at its best.*

give life in all its fullness" (John 10:10 TLB). Yet, for some this new relationship seems to dwindle down to just another stepping-stone in the pathway of frustration.

The Cycle

For the past thirty years I have witnessed a tragic phenomenon in my own life and in the lives of others. Instead of life being a process that leads from "glory to glory," from good to great, it is too often an incredibly frustrating cycle of ups and downs. For some the cycle ends in defeat, denial, or frustration. For too many, life is a series of ups and downs, a repetitive roller coaster from which they never recover. Every day counseling offices are filled with those who just can't seem to "pull it together" to find the longing of their heart.

This up-and-down cycle has dominated our lives for so long that we have unwittingly come to expect it. Religious leaders have created doctrines that justify it. Mental health care providers have given it medical names to make it seem like the norm. It is validated and even embraced in Christianity at large. We have tried everything from sin to super-achievement to numb the sting of its bite. Some have walked away from God. Others have blamed God. Still others have sunk into the world of denial. Regardless of the manner we choose to appease the beast, none of them brings us what we really want. We want the feeling of lack to go away! We want to be happy!

What we want is to live the life God promised. We want to have peace and joy. We want to live our dreams. We want our conscience free from guilt and shame. We want to face life without dread. We want to be free from the abiding sense of lack that drives us through life "by the sweat of our brow."

This is an age-old struggle. It did not begin with you. But it can end with you! You do not have to stay in the cycle. No matter where you are in the process, no matter how many times you have tried and failed, you can forever end the struggle of ups and downs. Your life can become a journey that takes you from one stage of victory to another, from good to great!

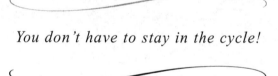

You don't have to stay in the cycle!

This book contains principles that will lead you to stability, peace, productivity, and endless joy. Read and ponder every word. Meditate on what you read. Open your heart and allow God to turn your life into an adventure of faith, love, and relationship. Allow every day to bring new joy and peace. Watch the problems that used to drag you hopelessly through the cycle fall away as you move into the life that God promised, the life that Jesus died and rose again to give you. Get your hope up one more time as you break the cycle and discover the unlimited power of faith righteousness. You will never be the same!

CHAPTER 2

THE SENSE OF LACK

One of the most unrealized promises of the New Testament is found in Colossians 2:10, when Paul boldly announced to those struggling believers, *"You are complete in Him, who is the head of all principality and power."* When a person feels lacking, inadequate, or incomplete, nothing seems farther from reality than this. But freedom from these feelings of inadequacy is a part of our heritage in Christ!

As with many New Covenant realities, there was a tremendous gap between what Jesus had given and what the people were experiencing. The Colossian believers were like most people. They had no concept of what it meant to experience the finished work of Jesus. They did not realize that His death, burial, and resurrection ensured them a life free from the penalty of sin. They didn't know that all the promises of God were assured for those who believe on the resurrected Jesus as Lord and Savior. Because they were not experiencing the reality of the finished work of Jesus, they became susceptible to "circumstance theology." Circumstance theology is simply the doctrinal position we create to justify or explain our current circumstance.

The church of Colosse, like most of the other churches addressed in the New Testament epistles, had slipped away from that place of completeness in Christ. Instead of interpreting their situation by the New Covenant, they began to interpret the New Covenant by their experience. This made them susceptible to the twisted doctrines of those who did not fully believe the finished work of Jesus. They had been seductively and systematically ushered into a sense of lack, and it took them back to the bondage of legalism and ritualism.

The Colossian believers had been influenced by teachers and prophets who brought them back under the slavery of dead works.[1] They no longer saw Christ as enough to qualify them for all the promises of God. They felt they were open prey for the devil if they did anything wrong. They actually thought they could lose their authority as a believer by failing to live up to the standards set by these so-called teachers.

A believer should never feel a sense of lack.
It should be foreign to our emotions
and contrary to our new nature in Christ.

They surrendered their faith to one of the most subtle, devastating, and controlling emotions known to man. They became enslaved to the sense of lack. This sense of need and desperation made them vulnerable to the manipulation of every type of false doctrine. They didn't *lose* the life and power of God when they accepted this feeling of lack; rather, they alienated themselves from the supernatural life of God that was in them. They reached a place where they could not access that power. Like Paul said of the Ephesians, they *"walk, in the futility of their mind, having their understanding darkened, being alienated from the life of God, because of the ignorance that is in them, because of the blindness of their heart"* (Ephesians 4:17–18).

A believer should never feel a sense of lack. It should be foreign to our emotions and contrary to our new nature in

---

1.   "Dead works" is a term used to describe the things we do to earn God's approval. The only thing that brings us God's approval is faith in the finished work of the Lord Jesus. This will be explained as you continue.

Christ. We should feel complete and whole. We should never be driven by the feelings of separation created by lack. No matter how real those feelings may be, no matter how undeserving we feel, it is not real! It is a vain imagination. It is a lie! It is a lie that has been used to manipulate mankind for thousands of years. It is the most powerful lie that one could believe. Yet, it is rampant in Christianity. It is woven into the fabric of mainstream theology. It surfaced within a few short years of the resurrection and has never gone away! Lack has been here so long it is considered normal. There are doctrines that explain why you should feel lack. There are even doctrines that would have you believe that God brings lack as a way to teach you. All these are contrary to everything we know about God's promises.

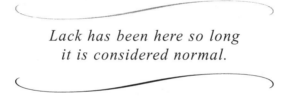

*Lack has been here so long
it is considered normal.*

Some would describe the sense of lack as low self-worth. Others may use the word *emptiness*. Still others would call it loneliness. Thousands of phobias and destructive emotional patterns, when reduced to their most basic feeling, are rooted in the sense of lack. That feeling is never from God! It is not how God motivates you. It is not how He leads you. In actuality, the sense of lack comes from not knowing, believing, and experiencing all that we have been freely given in Jesus.

*The sense of lack comes from not
knowing, believing, and experiencing
all that we have been freely given in Jesus.*

The Deceit of Lack

Since the Garden of Eden, man has been connected to the sense of lack. This is the emotion, whether subtle or overwhelming, that drives much of our decision-making. It is the feeling of lack that leads us to make desperate decisions that take us still farther away from our only true source of complete fulfillment. As a result, this sense of lack is a part of every dysfunction and is a precursor to nearly every pain we experience and sin we commit.

It all began in the Garden with a conversation between Eve and the serpent. Satan did not come straight out and attack God. That would have been too obvious. Neither did he immediately attempt to take Eve down a pathway to destruction. She would never have followed such an apparent ploy. Nor would you! No one gets up one day and decides, "I think I'll go out and commit some sin that will destroy my future and steal all my hopes and dreams."

Actually, just the opposite is true. Before we commit sin, we must first come to the place where we believe that sin will meet a need in our life. We don't commit sin to create problems. We commit sin to solve problems. The emotional state that so distorts our thinking is simply the state of lack. Before we look to sin to meet our need, we must first feel the need. We must have the feeling of lack!

Advertisers are masters at creating lack. Before they can sell us their products, they must first create the sense of lack. A master manipulator never creates lack with negatives. Quite the contrary, the sense of lack occurs when we are shown something we do not have, something desirable. The commercials show us the ideal man, the perfect woman, or the house of our dreams. They show the average person experiencing these perfect outcomes and then they show us a perfume, a lending institution, or even a cigarette. A subtle connection is made between smoking their brand and having this great experience. In the end we are made to feel that if we do not use their product we can never have the "promise." This feeling of lack—the desire to have the dream house or the search for the perfect mate—is associated with their product.

We don't commit sin to create problems. We commit sin to solve problems. The emotional state that so distorts our thinking is simply the state of lack.

In other words, they make us feel a sense of lack, then they offer us a solution. They have to sell the need before they can sell us their product. They get us "hooked," then offer the fix! Advertising is actually designed to create codependency. Codependency is when we look outside of ourselves to meet a need that only God Himself can meet in our heart.

This is the primary strategy of political campaigns. They tell us how bad the country has become. They create a picture in our minds of how bad it will grow to be. They fill our hearts with fear (need), and then they offer to protect us from the evil of which they have persuaded us to believe. They make us feel needy and then offer themselves as the solution.

Satan simply asked Eve a few strategic questions. Questions are powerful tools. They have the ability to lead us down paths we would never choose otherwise. We have to be careful what questions we ask ourselves. If we ask the wrong questions, we always reach the wrong conclusions. Satan doesn't need you to deny Jesus in order to destroy you. All he needs is for you to believe that what Jesus has given is not enough. The moment you believe there is one thing that God has not given you through the death, burial, and resurrection of Jesus, you connect to the sense of lack.

The church has been systematically trained to ask the wrong questions. Most of our questions are based on the presumption of lack. We do not really believe in the promises that come to us through the finished work of Jesus. Instead, we view His promises as a work in progress, as something that is based more on our actions than on His. From this basis of lack,

Satan doesn't need you to deny Jesus in order to destroy you. All he needs is for you to believe that what Jesus has given is not enough.

we sincerely seek to solve our problems while creating more pain and frustration. Thus most of our attempts to discover freedom and victory take us farther from the truth. The more committed and genuine we are, the more we are susceptible to this type of subtle destruction.

The Truth Is, We Are Complete in Jesus

When our beliefs are not based on the completed work of Jesus, we do not connect with the fact that *we are complete in Jesus!* Instead we start from the position that says, "I am not complete in Jesus." Starting from that theological and emotional basis, every question we ask ourselves, every decision we make, leads us farther from victory. It takes us in a cycle of religion[2] and dead works wherein there is no victory, only disappointment and failure.

Eve believed a lie. She believed there was something that God had not done for her, thereby alienating herself from the life of God. She abandoned the promises and power that had made it possible for her to live in paradise. Her beliefs drove her emotions, and her emotions drove her actions. The moment Eve believed the lie of lack, she began to be driven by fear instead of faith. Fear became a self-fulfilling prophecy that validated her seductive feelings.

---

2. Religion is man's attempt to know and please God apart from the finished work of Jesus. Faith, on the other hand, is trust in what Jesus did through His death, burial, and resurrection.

Once our feelings are validated, we begin to trust those feelings more than the realities of God. Our emotions become *lying vanities that cause us to forsake our own mercies.*[3] We are now in the cycle! Like a wind-up toy that runs in circles, our life's patterns are set. We will never break out of the cycle until we turn back to the truth of God's Word.

All of Paul's writings were focused on bringing the believer back to the finished work of Jesus, back to our new identity in Him, back to the foundation of the Gospel: faith righteousness. When your sense of wholeness and completeness, that is, your feeling of righteousness, is based on the finished work of Jesus, you are immovable. You are established. You are standing on the rock! You are free from the power of lack!

When your sense of wholeness and completeness,
that is, your feeling of righteousness, is based
on the finished work of Jesus, you are immovable.

Are you connected to the sense of lack or do you consistently experience wholeness? If you are not sure, here are some simple things you can do to determine the answer to this question. Find a quiet place. Settle your mind. Have your Bible, pen, and paper at hand. Pick out a few scriptures about completeness in Jesus. Quote them aloud, being sure to personalize them and stating them in the present tense.

You may want to use the scripture from Colossians 2:10: *"You are complete in Him, who is the head of all principality and power."* Simply state, "I am complete in Jesus. I lack nothing." Now sit quietly and see what thoughts or feelings come to mind. Write them down. These reflect your emotional reaction to this vital truth. You can do this with any scripture that promises you something through Christ.

---

3.   Jonah 2:8: *"They that observe lying vanities forsake their own mercy"* (KJV).

Another thing you can do is look at a picture of yourself. Then write down your first reactions to what you see. If your first response is negative, then you are probably connected to a sense of lack. Lack, rather than confidence and faith, is driving your decision-making. But you can change all of that forever. Take a few moments to pray. Let God know that you are willing to open your heart to a whole new sense of self. Commit yourself to establishing an entirely new sense of identity in Jesus. Now hold on for the ride of your life! The journey out of lack will be the best decision you have ever made!

CHAPTER 3

NAKED AND VULNERABLE

Once we buy into the lie of lack, we become vulnerable to every kind of temptation and emotional manipulation. The feeling of need leads us to believe that Jesus did not, in fact, complete the work of redemption; therefore, His other promises of peace and joy cannot become a reality. Once we believe this lie, we spend all of our energies struggling with those things over which Jesus said we had been given the victory. Our every attempt at faith becomes a false reinforcement that His Word is not true. We become trapped in the cycle of lack.

As far as we know, Adam and Eve had never faced any temptation until they started answering the wrong questions. "Is this really what God said? Did He actually mean this?" Once the environment of emotional lack was created, they lost their connection to their sense of identity and relationship with God. Their perception changed. The way they experienced life changed. They felt lack even though there was no lack. Now they were at a place where blatant accusations could be railed against God—accusations that felt true but were in fact completely false.

Such is the plight of people trapped in the cycle. They start out questioning the surety of the promises of God. Ultimately they begin to question other aspects of the finished work of Jesus. All of this leads to feelings of lack and uncertainty. In the end, they abandon the promises of God and set out to find happiness through their own means, independent of God. If the cycle of ups and downs continues, they blame God and openly attack Him. What started as simply asking the wrong questions ends in outright defiance. This is what happened in the Garden of Eden. Once Adam and Eve connected to the sense of lack, Satan could openly challenge God.

"For God knows that when you eat of it your eyes will be opened, and you will be like God," Satan charged in Genesis 3:5 (NIV). The absurdity of this accusation lies in the fact that they were already like God. When God created man, He said, *"Let us make man in our image, after our likeness: and let them have dominion"* (Genesis 1:26). Man was created in the image of God and made ruler over the earth. He lacked nothing. He lived in perfect harmony with God and the environment. Nothing could have improved the quality of his life.

True completeness comes from the sense of who you are, not from what you possess or what you can accomplish. At the heart of this temptation was the implication, "You are not who God says you are. Therefore, you do not have what God says you have." The only way to believe you could become more is to feel lack. The only reason to want more is to sense lack! The attempt to become more righteous is proof that you do not believe you are righteous in Jesus. The commitment to become sanctified is a testimony to the fact that you do not believe you have been sanctified. The person who believes he or she is a new creation in Jesus never pursues the destructive process of

True completeness comes from the sense of who you are, not from what you possess or what you can accomplish.

becoming. Instead, these believers reinforce the fact that they are, they have, and they can in Jesus. They look to the work Jesus finished instead of to the work they will finish.

Need is a lesser expression of addiction.
It takes us where we never thought we would go.

Lack makes you the center of every equation. Faith, on the other hand, makes Jesus the center. When in the state of lack, we abandon God's promises and enter the deceitful world of religion. In this world of "smoke and mirrors," we never quite live up to the standards that others impose on us. We always feel inadequate. Our image of God and the world is distorted and negative. Our life becomes driven by need instead of satisfaction. Need is a lesser expression of addiction. It takes us where we never thought we would go.

The Illogic of Lack

We don't know how long Adam and Eve lived in the Garden. Neither do we know how many times they walked past the tree of the knowledge of good and evil. We also have no record of them ever being enticed to eat of the tree until they had succumbed to the sense of lack. Until that time, they had no compelling desire to violate God's word.

Afterwards, however, in this state of emotional insanity (lack), the entire world looked different. That which never had any appeal to this royal family now was like honey to the hungry. It now became the object of their desire. They were obsessed by the illusion of completeness that could be experienced only by partaking of the luscious fruit. The Message Bible says it like this: *"When the Woman saw that the tree looked like good eating and realized what she would get out it...she took and ate the fruit"* (Genesis 3:6). The false expectation of a fulfillment that would meet an imaginary need led her to commit an act that would forever change the course of human history.

What could have possibly led her to such an inaccurate logic? The sense of lack! In the state of lack, that which we would normally run away from now compels us. That which we would normally detest becomes our delight. That which we would consider only under the cover of darkness becomes our open pursuit. Why? It all looks so appealing in the state of lack! *"So when the woman saw that the tree was good for food, that it was pleasant to the eyes, and a tree desirable to make one wise, she took of its fruit and ate. She also gave to her husband with her, and he ate"* (Genesis 3:6).

> *In the state of lack, that which we would normally run away from now compels us.*

This is the same power that leads a lonely person to lie about his or her life to gain acceptance. It will cause a person who is feeling rejected at home to commit adultery. It will make sin a logical and compelling choice.

The power of temptation is simply the power of desire. Actually, every temptation emerges from a God-given need. Temptation is the not the appeal to do what we do not want to do. It is the longing for a desire to be fulfilled. But when we feel inadequate and unqualified, we see no hope of fulfilling our longings in a God-given manner. Therefore we turn to back to *"the weak and beggarly elements"* that take us back to bondage.[1]

Just as Adam and Eve had a sense of nakedness, we too feel vulnerable and naked because of the abiding sense of lack. As a result, we attempt to conquer temptation by attacking the

---

1. Galatians 4:9: *"But now after you have known God, or rather are known by God, how is it that you turn again to the weak and beggarly elements, to which you desire again to be in bondage?"*

external. We make new rules and laws that should lead us to perfection but instead take us deeper into the feelings of lack. We ignore the truth that says that laws can only make us aware of our failures. They can in no way give us power over sin. Paul said, *"By the deeds of the law no flesh will be justified in His sight, for by the law is the knowledge of sin"* (Romans 3:20).

Why would we do something that the Bible clearly says would in no way bring us freedom? That's simple; it's the logic of lack! Just as lack rendered the understanding of Adam and Eve devoid of sound judgment, so it creates a cloud of confusion. It makes simple truth seem vague and uncertain. We do just as Satan suggested and make ourselves to be god of our own world. Our logic becomes the *logos* wherein we look for salvation and deliverance.

We make more rules so we can get out of sin, but instead it takes us deeper into sin. The very thing we did to bring us life instead brings us death.

As lack leads us into more faulty logic, we make even more rules. We make them harder and more demanding, all the while becoming more vulnerable to sin. Our logic just cannot see the wisdom of God's Word that says, *"The strength of sin is the law"* (1 Corinthians 15:56). Can you image such a twisted and discouraging fate? We make more rules so we can get out of sin, but instead it takes us deeper into sin. The very thing we did to bring us life instead brings us death. All the while the feeling of lack and inadequacy grows deeper. Our sense of being qualified before God sinks to an undetectable level. As a result, we cannot trust a God who in our mind has no value for us.

To Put It in a Nutshell...

God created us to live in paradise. He gifted us with God-given desires that should be discovered and realized as we walk in harmony with Him. Yet, the very desires that should draw us to Him—our Source of ultimate fulfillment—lead us away from Him through our faulty logic of lack. Through our destructive pursuit of happiness we encounter all manner of pain. Then, mired in deceit, we assume that the pain is God punishing us for trying to find happiness.

The reality of this cycle became evident as I counseled with a dear young woman who found herself continually in moral compromise. She never believed that she could be sexually gratified if she lived in a monogamous relationship. Her feelings of lack led her to believe that God would not give her the best life has to offer. She didn't realize that trying to fulfill a God-given desire in an ungodly way would always lead to undesirable results. She felt that God was keeping her from the fulfillment for which she longed.

Attempting to fulfill our desires through sin is like trying to fulfill an addiction through drugs. Every time we commit the sin, it makes us less capable of experiencing joy. Instead, the need grows deeper. Therefore, the sense of lack drives us to commit the sin again. And the more we sin, the more we need to sin as we attempt to gratify our desires.

*Attempting to fulfill our desires through sin
is like trying to fulfill an addiction through drugs.*

What do you believe? Do you feel that God wants you to be happy and fulfilled? Or do you feel drawn to ungodly means for meeting some of your most basic desires? Do you feel drawn away because you don't believe there is a godly way to satisfy these desires? Or do you feel unqualified for God to meet those needs?

No matter where you may find yourself in the addiction to lack, you can start the process of recovery. You can make the first and most essential decision right at this moment. If you are willing to believe that God's Word is true—whether you understand it or not—you have taken the first and most essential step. When your emotions are inconsistent with the Word of God, you must remind yourself, "These feeling are real, but they are not based on reality." Then pray, "Father, I acknowledge Your Word as truth, and I trust that You will lead me into all truth. You are my Shepherd, and I shall not lack. I base this confidence on the finished work of Jesus."

This simple decision to exalt God's Word above your experience will set you on the road of recovery from lack and launch you into a life of wholeness!

CHAPTER 4

IDENTITY RECOVERED

Thousands of years after the first Adam lost his sense of identity in the Garden of Eden and surrendered to the "lie of lack," Jesus, whom the Bible describes as the second Adam, faced the identical struggle. The first Adam lost all that man had been given by God. Jesus, the second Adam, came to recover all that we lost and give us more than we had ever known.

In Matthew 4 Jesus encountered the first major battle that stood between Him and His destiny. He, like us, had to resolve the issue of identity before He could move on to fulfill God's plan for His life. This is the initial struggle that defines our destiny. The outcome of this one battle will either launch us into lack and the raging cycle of destruction or will set us on the course of faith and fulfillment.

The sense of identity is the very foundation upon which all our hopes and dreams lie. We will live our destiny only to the degree that we live in an abiding sense of who we are in Jesus. Over two hundred times the New Testament utilizes what I call "identity scriptures." These are scriptures that refer to who we are "in Him," "through Him," or "by Him." Plus,

We will live our destiny only to the degree that we live in an abiding sense of who we are in Jesus.

there are references to "what we have" or "what we can do" because of Him. We must accept these truths as our new identity and live from this source of confidence and power. In the Garden, Adam originally ruled the world out of his sense of identity. He knew who he was in relation to God. He had no other sense of self. The Bible says that he was created to be like God. He was crowned with glory and honor.[1]

The words *glory* and *honor* also could be translated as "dignity" and "worth." "Glory and honor" in Psalm 8 is not a symbolic reference to some vague religious concept. This was the emotional crown man wore. It was his abiding sense of self. He had a sense of dignity and worth based on who he was in relation to his Creator! As long as man maintained that sense of identity, he ruled planet Earth. He lived his destiny in effortless bliss!

Man did not lose his dominion over planet Earth when he fell. He lost his sense of identity. He still ruled Earth. He did not, however, rule out of dignity and worth. Instead of ruling from a sense of wholeness, he ruled from fear and lack. It is the sense of fear and lack that drives man to seek power through control. Power and force become a demoralizing substitute for authority and leadership. When Adam sinned, fear and unbelief replaced faith and love as the dominant emotional quality of man. Yet, man still had a sense of destiny. He longed to be who God said he was. He longed to live the way he was created to live. But now he sought that destiny driven by something that would oppose every God-instilled attribute: fear and lack.

Jesus could not launch into His ultimate destiny, He could not step into His public ministry, and He certainly could not face death on the cross until He was immovable in

---

1.   Psalm 8:4–6: "*What is man that You are mindful of him, and the son of man that You visit him? For You have made him a little lower than the angels, and You have crowned him with glory and honor. You have made him to have dominion over the works of Your hands; You have put all things under his feet.*"

His identity as the Son of God. His ability to face the obstacles of the ministry, His commitment to a life of service and sacrifice arose out of a sense of who He was in relationship to God. John 13:3–5 shows us the source of His inner strength. *"Jesus, knowing that the Father had given all things into His hands, and that He had come from God and was going to God, rose from supper…to wash the disciples' feet."* As Jesus' death on the cross and

*Jesus could not face death
on the cross until He was immovable
in His identity as the Son of God.*

rejection from God drew near, He remained the humble, obedient servant. The secret to His power and composure lay in His knowledge of who He was. He was never compelled to prove His identity by exerting power. He never used the people around Him for His purposes. His sense of wholeness freed Him to live as a servant until the end.

God wants our walk in this world to be founded on our sense of restored identity in Jesus. He desires us to live in that sense of dignity and worth, of glory and honor. Jesus modeled the essential value for this cornerstone characteristic on the mount of temptation.

*God wants our walk in this world to be
founded on our sense of restored identity in Jesus.*

How to Answer the Wrong Question

Just as Satan had approached Adam and Eve in the Garden, he came to Jesus asking questions—the wrong questions,

questions designed to lead Him to the wrong conclusions. He asked the same strategic questions that would cause people who are not firmly established in their sense of identity to reach the false feeling of lack. *"Now when the tempter came to Him, he said, 'If You are the Son of God, command that these stones become bread' "* (Matthew 4:3).

Satan did not refute the fact that Jesus was the Son of God. One translation reads, "Since you are God's Son."[2] Then, what is so wrong with this question? Why didn't Jesus simply work a miracle to prove who He was? Satan, in his subtle mind game, was asking Jesus to prove His identity by His performance. The need to perform to prove always comes from the sense of lack.

Had Jesus wavered in His sense of identity through relationship with God, had He followed the logic of the question, had He started asking Himself the wrong questions, He would have started down a path of works righteousness that would have led to His fall. His life would have become consumed with proving His identity instead of living His identity.

*The need to perform to prove
always comes from the sense of lack.*

The main message the devil has for you—the message of all codependent teaching, the message of religion, the message that lies at the core of everything that has robbed the church of victory—is the charge, "You are not who God says you are. Therefore you do not have what God says you have." It is this very idea that leads us into desperate codependent behavior. It is this belief that alienates us, in our mind, from the life and promises of God that have been freely given to us in Jesus.

---

2.   The Message Bible

The question may not come to us in the same manner that it came to Jesus. For us it may be presented in the form of qualification. "What is it that actually qualifies me for the promises of God? What qualifies me to go to heaven? What qualifies me to receive a miracle in my time of need? Why should God answer my prayers? Or, most importantly, why should God love me?" After all, we reason, He could surely find fault with us! Focusing on our fault, however, connects us to the sense of lack.

The main message the devil has for you is the charge, "You are not who God says you are. Therefore you do not have what God says you have."

The Gospel leads people away from the sense of lack that comes from personal fault. *"Yet now He has reconciled in the body of His flesh through death, to present you holy, and blameless, and above reproach in His sight"* (Colossians 1:21–22). The Amplified Bible says we stand *"faultless and irreproachable."* The New Living Translation says, *"blameless...without a single fault."* God's view of us, in Christ, is drastically different than our view of ourselves. His view connects us to wholeness and confidence. Our view connects us to fear and lack!

We, through our logic of lack, look at our faults and then to the conditions of the Old Covenant and say, "My faults separate me from God." However, the New Covenant says nothing can separate us from the love of God in Christ Jesus. *"For I am persuaded that neither death nor life, nor angels nor principalities nor powers, nor things present nor things to come, nor height nor depth, nor any other created thing, shall be able to separate us from the love of God which is in Christ Jesus our Lord"* (Romans 8:38–39).

Paul said that wicked works had the power to make you feel alienated from God. That alienation is not real, however.

It is only a feeling, even though it feels real! It is that sense of lack, although completely false, that drives an imaginary, emotional wedge between you and God. *"And you, who once were alienated and enemies in your mind by wicked works, yet now He has reconciled"* (Colossians 1:21). Jesus was hungry from fasting. He was in fact tempted to give in to Satan's ploy. However, instead of creating a doctrine based on circumstance, He went back to what the Word of God says. He did not assume that because He was hungry God had abandoned Him. He did not make the satisfying of His hunger the proof that He was accepted by God. He rested in who He was, the Son of God.

Deserving or Qualified?

If we ask ourselves the wrong question, we end up like Adam and Eve: alienated from God through the fear and unbelief in our mind. We usually ask ourselves if we are worthy enough for God to answer our prayers or meet our needs. The answer to that is an obvious NO! But God doesn't answer our prayers and fulfill His Word because we are worthy; He does it because we are qualified. There is a difference. I may not be worthy based on my actions. But I am qualified for all the promises of God because I am in Jesus! To be qualified is to meet the legal requirements. To be worthy is to be deserving. I meet the legal requirements even when I am personally undeserving. Why? Because I am in Jesus! He is worthy!

God doesn't answer our prayers and fulfill His Word because we are worthy; He does it because we are qualified.

Paul said it this way: *"Giving thanks to the Father who has qualified us to be partakers of the inheritance of the saints in the light"* (Colossians 1:12). How could I possibly be qualified when I am not worthy? Simple! Jesus is worthy. He inherited all the promises of God. I am now in Christ. In Him I share in all the inheritance, all the riches of God.

In Jesus we were all given the gift of righteousness. We do not stand before God in our righteousness. We stand before Him in the righteousness of Christ Himself! *"But now the righteousness of God without the law is manifested, being witnessed by the law and the prophets; even the righteousness of God which is by faith of Jesus Christ unto all and upon all them that believe: for there is no difference"* (Romans 3:21–22).

We have a righteousness that is not of our making. It is not based on our performance; it is based in the finished work of the Lord Jesus. *"But of him are ye in Christ Jesus, who of God is made unto us wisdom, and righteousness, and sanctification, and redemption"* (1 Corinthians 1:30).

We do not stand before God in our righteousness.
We stand before Him in the righteousness of Christ Himself.

When we receive His righteousness as a free gift, our conscience is made clear and our sense of self changes. We step into the identity that man was created to enjoy—one of dignity and worth. It is this very sense of righteousness that gives us peace and frees us from fear of wrath. It is the righteousness of Jesus that frees us from the abiding sense of lack, doom, low self-worth, and the vague feeling of not measuring up. It is in this spiritual/emotional state that we fulfill our God-given destiny as priests and kings.

What is the source of your identity? The way you answer the following questions will help you understand whether your confidence and faith is based on your identity in Jesus or if your identity is based on your performance.

What do you believe qualifies you to go to heaven?

Do you believe that being in Jesus is enough to qualify you for all the promises of God?

What do you believe qualifies you for the love of God?

When things go wrong in your life, is your first reaction to wonder why God let it happen? Do you become introspective to see what you have done wrong?

When you pray, do you find yourself going through a mental checklist of successes and sins to determine if God will answer your prayer?

When you ask yourself these questions, be sure to watch yourself. Don't let these questions lead you down the wrong path. Make Jesus the answer to each of these questions. Make Him your total and complete confidence for every qualification and every promise. As you make Him your focus, your sense of peace and confidence will cease to vacillate. You will experience confidence and assurance that is beyond your own understanding! You will discover what it means to be "in Him"!

CHAPTER 5

DRIVEN BY LACK

As the young woman sat before me, crying, with her face in her hands, I felt such compassion. At the same time, I knew she had to face a cruel reality or be plunged mercilessly back into the religious cycle of lack and defeat. Her dialogue vacillated from anger and shame to justification and defensiveness. Things had not turned out the way she had planned. She insisted that she wanted to serve God. However, every opportunity she had been given to serve turned into a problem.

She was one of those people who just conveyed something negative. Granted, she was more than willing to come and give her time. She used all the right "buzz words" about wanting to serve God. But she seemed to exude something unhealthy. Dysfunctional people were drawn to her and healthy people were somewhat repelled by her.

With her mouth she expressed a desire to serve. Yet, the unspoken message that she sent to everyone around her was, "I don't want to be here!" Now, as she sat in my office, it was time for her to come to grips with the conflicting message and mixed signals. We wanted her to have a legitimate opportunity, but we could not allow her to continue to bring disruption.

She had come from a church background where great emphasis was placed on "serving." Well, I guess you couldn't really call it serving. Serving is what one does voluntarily, for the benefit of the recipient. What she had grown up with would have been more like slavery. Slavery is when you are forced to do something for the benefit of the one who oppresses and controls you.

She had never been able to feel right about herself in our church. She was glad to be free from the control, but she didn't really know how to function in an environment free from manipulation. Intellectually we were in full agreement. Yet, emotionally she was unhappy. I asked her to step out of "serving" for a while to work through the issues. I felt she needed to step away and identify her motivation. She was angry at me for asking her to take a break, but she had exuded even more anger when she was given the opportunity to serve. This contradiction was not uncommon for those who came to us from "high-pressure churches."

We had attempted to work through this with her before to no avail. But today's conversation had touched too many emotions to let it go unresolved. She was crying, not because I had asked her to step down from her position; she was crying because I had asked her the question, "Why do you really want to do all the things you do? Is it because you love God? Is it because you love the people? If love is motivating you, why do you express so many negative emotions?" She could not honestly give an affirmative answer to those questions.

Finally, in an explosion of emotion, she blurted out, "I did all those things to get God to love me." My suspicions were finally confirmed. She was driven by lack, not love. She didn't want to do what she was doing, but it was the only way she knew to feel accepted of God. Obligation had replaced love. She was meeting *her* need, not the needs of the people.

Like so many, this young woman did not recognize what was really driving her actions. It was not the love of God motivating her. It was unbelief in the love of God. It was not really the desire to serve, but the fear of not serving that moved her to action. God does not drive you! He leads you. We do not follow Him out of fear. We follow Him because we trust Him. He is our shepherd not our tyrant.

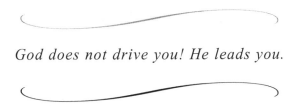

God does not drive you! He leads you.

In the Amplified Bible, Psalm 23 boldly declares, *"The Lord is my Shepherd...I shall not lack."* The Message Bibles says it like this: *"God, my shepherd! I don't need a thing."* This entire psalm gives us a picturesque description of the person who trustingly follows God as his shepherd. Such followers are freed from lack. They rest in green pastures and when in dangerous places they experience peace and protection. Only goodness and mercy pursue them. They aren't driven. They are led. Fear is not the dominant emotion. Peace is.

Love and peace are a breeding ground for productive service. Fear and lack can produce activity, but productivity is low and conflict is high. The person driven to service through fear has no joy in serving. In actuality, a person driven by fear should not serve. He first should discover God's love for him as a son, not a servant.

Son or Slave?

Paul told the Galatians, *"Because you are sons, God sent the Spirit of his Son into our hearts, the Spirit who calls out, 'Abba, Father' "* (Galatians 4:6 NIV). God didn't create mankind to be slaves. He had angels to do His bidding. He didn't create us to be an army. He had angels to fight His battles. He created us to be family. When man violated his relationship with God, he became sinful in nature. He lost the sense of family. He was no longer sustained by the sense of dignity and worth. Instead, he became driven by fear and lack. In his own religious mind he could be no more than a slave to a holy, perfect God.

In Galatians 4:8 Paul said, *"Formerly, when you did not know God, you were slaves..."* (NIV). All we have ever known is slavery. We were slaves to our passions and desires. Religious people who have not been born again are slaves to rules, rituals, and regulations. As a result, we bring our slave mentality to God and interpret Him from our own skewed perception.

We consider God to be a taskmaster who must be pleased by our loyal service. We don't believe that Jesus qualified us for all the promises of God through His death, burial, and resurrection, so in slave-like attitude we set out to earn what has been freely given to become what God has already empowered us to be. In verse 7 of the same chapter Paul said, *"So you are no longer a slave, but a son; and since you are a son, God has made you also an heir"* (NIV).

As an heir we receive all things based on the promise, the covenant. We freely receive what we could not earn. We inherit what works and performance could not deliver. We become a part of a family with full rights, privileges, and a complete inheritance. In Galatians 4:5 Paul said Jesus came, *"to redeem them that were under the law, that we might receive the adoption of sons"* (KJV). We were not bought as slaves. We were adopted as son, with all rights and privileges.

A son doesn't wonder about his standing in the family. A slave has to prove his worth every day. A son doesn't have to earn the inheritance. It will become his through the love and generosity of the father. A son knows that all the father has is his. A slave never owns anything and has no sense of security.

What happened to the Galatians that they lost this sense? These believers had come under the control of a group of religious people called the Judaizers. This was a group of people who believed that Jesus was the Messiah, but they did not believe He could make the believer righteous. Therefore, they told people that they had to observe religious traditions and keep the Law of Moses as a way to earn God's blessing and have protection from the devil. They connected people with the sense of lack. They turned sons into slaves. They took the inheritance and made it payment for works performed. They infected others with their own sense of lack.

Just as fear and lack perverted Adam's view of God, these Galatian believers who once experienced freedom and peace through Jesus now changed their view of God and felt unworthy and unqualified. When the sense of lack prevails, we feel like slaves and call God "Master." When the spirit of sonship prevails, we feel like sons and call God "Father." When we are

When the sense of lack prevails, we feel like slaves and call God "Master." When the spirit of sonship prevails, we feel like sons and call God "Father."

connected to completeness, we have the sense of all our needs being met. When we are connected to a sense of slavery, we try to earn from God. Paul said it like this:

> *For you did not receive the spirit of bondage again to fear, but you received the Spirit of adoption by whom we cry out, "Abba, Father." The Spirit Himself bears witness with our spirit that we are children of God, and if children, then heirs—heirs of God and joint heirs with Christ* (Romans 8:15–17).

Paul boldly pointed out the motivation of those who would reduce the children of God to a slave mentality: control! Listen to the way it reads in the Message Bible: *"Those heretical teachers go to great lengths to flatter you, but their motives are rotten. They want to shut you out of the free world of God's grace so that you will always depend on them for approval and direction, making them feel important"* (Galatians 4:17).

Paul compared this seduction to witchcraft when he said, *"O foolish Galatians! Who has bewitched you?"* (Galatians 3:1) Witchcraft is an act of putting a spell on a person in order to gain control of his life. Connecting to the sense of lack is like having someone put a spell on us and take control of our lives. People who sense lack always give up control of their life to someone or something.

The Judaizers gained control by undermining the believers' trust in the finished work of Jesus. Then they began to dole out the list of commandments, rituals, and cultural observances that must be adhered to as a means of obtaining God's approval (and theirs). They became a substitute for the voice of God in the heart of the believer. They had them ready to go to any length to serve God as a slave.

When people who are sincere about knowing God are connected to lack, they will go to any length to find a sense of God's love and presence. A hunger for God must be matched by the knowledge of truth or it will become a driving force that leads away from God and into slavery. Proverbs 19:2 says, *"It is not good to have zeal without knowledge, nor to be hasty and miss the way"* (NIV).

Motivation for Service

Paul was a fervent, passionate servant of God. He was very clear about his motivation: He was not driven by fear and lack. He was not attempting to earn approval or privileges. He was compelled by love. In Romans 1:1 (KJV), as well as many places through the Scriptures, Paul referred to himself as a *servant* of the Lord Jesus. The original language would translate it more as a bondservant. One of the root Greek words means to bind. Kenneth Wuest says this refers to one who is bound to another. Wuest goes on to say, "The word refers to one whose will is swallowed up in another."[1]

---

1.   Kenneth S. Wuest, *Word Studies in the Greek New Testament*, Vol. III (Grand Rapids, Michigan: Wm. B. Eerdmans Publishing Company, 1968), 45.

Paul made it clear that it was not fear or bondage that brought about his commitment to serve God. It was sonship. Like the love slaves of the Old Testament, our debt has been paid. We are free from the penalty of sin. The law now has no power over us. What will we do with this newfound freedom? The love slave was so overcome with love and gratitude for his previous master that he was compelled to serve that master the rest of his life out of choice. Love compelled him to do what no debt could produce: absolute, total commitment.

Because of our sin, we had a debt to the law. The law required that every infraction be paid for with our life. Jesus, however, died to free us from the debt of punishment. He was raised up to provide us with righteousness to qualify us for all the promises. Appreciation for what He has done should be the motivating response for all we do for Him.

In Colossians 3:12–13 Paul listed all sorts of positive attributes that should define the life of the believer. *"Therefore, as the elect of God, holy and beloved, put on tender mercies, kindness, humility, meekness, longsuffering; bearing with one another, and forgiving one another, if anyone has a complaint against another; even as Christ forgave you."* All of these actions could emerge from unhealthy beliefs and attitudes. We could be merciful because of the fear of rejection. Our kindness could be compelled by codependency. Our meekness could be the fruit of low self-worth. But Paul made it clear that the one thing that binds all the Christian life and virtues together is love. *"And over all these virtues put on love, which binds them all together in perfect unity"* (Colossians 3:14 NIV). Love should motivate every aspect of our Christian life. The right action driven by a sense of lack never produces good fruit.

Every person should ask himself, "Why do I do the good things I do?" We must determine if our life is motivated by love or fear. Is God a shepherd whom we trust fully to lead us to every good aspect of life? Or are we driven by fear and lack?

What is the fruit of our service to God? Is it peace and joy, or is it frustration and anger? For the next week, every time you do anything good for anyone, or when you do anything in relationship to God, simply ask, "Why am I doing this?" Discover what's driving your life.

The right action driven by a sense of lack never produces good fruit.

If you discover you are being driven by negative emotions, it does not mean you must stop what you are doing. Simply remind yourself that God loves you because you are a son (or daughter). Acknowledge that Jesus has qualified you for all God's promises. Now determine that you will do what you do for the good of the people you serve.

By adjusting your focus, you will find new joy in serving. Your emotions will change and your physical energy will increase. Although serving does not buy you anything from God, it does facilitate the opportunity to have insights into God that will bring you incredible amounts of fulfillment like you've never had.

CHAPTER 6

THE QUALIFYING FACTOR

W hen I called on Jesus to save and deliver me, my life was a mess. I knew I needed His love and power to change my life. I could not do it alone. Up until that moment, it didn't matter where I lived, who I was with, or what I did, there was always trouble. After changing my name, living under an alias, traveling from city to city searching for adventure, and still finding myself in the same problems over and over again, I knew that *I* was my problem.

A few years ago county singer Clint Black came out with a song that said, "Wherever you go, there you are." Nothing could be more true! That had been my problem—I could not escape from me. For many years I numbed the emptiness through substance abuse. I was able to bury the pain of an un-fulfilled life under the blur of intoxication. But as the power of the drugs waned, I needed something stronger, something more permanent. Suicide began to call.

I would take extreme amounts of drugs and get as close to the edge of death as I could. But even in the midst of that, there was always another voice calling. I believe it was the voice of God. No matter how close I got to the edge there was always that "other voice" that kept calling me back and giving me hope.

Late one night after my wife had gone to bed, I got as high as I could and still function. I went out to the edge of the four-lane street that ran in front of my house. I stood on the curb waiting for a car to come by. I had decided that I would finally break free from me. By stepping in front of the next car I would end this life of personal torment. I would make the final escape—death.

As I stood waiting, the words to a song began to float up into my consciousness. The haunting lyrics asked, "Is that all there is?" I saw myself dead, immersed in complete darkness, separated from God. Again I heard the words of the song, "Is that all there is?" I had the sudden realization that my pain would not end in death. If I died without knowing God, I would be eternally buried in pain with no hope of ever finding relief. The sudden fear was sobering.

I renewed my search for God. For years I had tried to find God. I prayed every night. I just wanted to know Him. I wanted Him to bring me the relief for which I so desperately longed. I went to churches and talked to preachers, but no one gave me the simple Gospel. I had preachers affirm that I was going to hell. Still others told me no one was going to hell, so I shouldn't worry about it. I knew that neither of these extremes held hope for me. I was determined to find the God who was calling out in my heart.

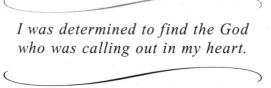

*I was determined to find the God
who was calling out in my heart.*

One day a friend shared his criticisms of a relative who had recently witnessed to him. Amidst the criticism and profanity, I was able to get enough truth to recognize where I was in relation to God. I let him out of my car and began to pray. I finally had enough truth to know what to do. Even though it came through words of criticism laced with profanity, it was still truth. And it still had the power to save!

That day I realized that God had found me. He had been looking for me my whole life. It was His voice that had called out to me as a child that gave me the hope of a better life. It was His voice that called me back from the edge of death so many times. It was Him who had never given up. However, it wasn't until I accepted Him on His terms that I was able to experience the reality of the new birth and an empowered life.

That day, in an instant, I was delivered from a lifetime of lack—the lack of a loving father, the lack of a nurturing childhood, the lack that was attached to a life of sin. I was delivered from lack by uniting with, wrapping my life around, and fully committing myself to Jesus as my Lord.[1] Just as light drives out darkness, a heart that is alive to Jesus as Lord cannot be alive to lack.

The old me died! I finally found a way to kill the old me that I had grown to despise, yet still go on living. The words of Paul, which I later read, made complete sense: *"I am crucified with Christ: nevertheless I live"* (Galatians 2:20 KJV). I found a chance at a new life. And that is what I wanted. I wanted to be free from me and for the first time I was. I wanted a better life, and now it was mine!

I had done nothing more than believe and act on the truth. I had not earned anything. Without any qualifications on my part I experienced the greatest miracle of all, the new birth. Peace flooded my heart. A sense of knowing and certainty that I had never known girded me. I had a revelation of the love of God that was beyond expression. To this day I cannot put into words what I experienced in that car so long ago.

I was immediately empowered to live as I chose. Now, when I chose to say no to drugs, I had the power to see that

---

1. When we believe what Jesus did for us through His death, burial, and resurrection, we must determine if He is worthy to be trusted with our life. To trust and follow Him is a commitment to His Lordship.

decision through. When I chose to be kind or to face conflict, I was empowered to do so. I was no longer drug through life by out-of-control emotions. The fear and insecurity that had driven my life was gone. I knew that I was a different person.

I did not immediately go to church. Instead, I went home, poured out all my drugs and alcohol, dug around until I found a Bible, and began to read. By the time I went to church I had read all of the New Testament. I was praying with fervency. None of this was the product of obligation; it was the product of passion. I was in love and I wanted to know this Person who had done so much for me.

What Churches Had to Say

A few weeks later when I went to church for the first time, I walked down the aisle and made a public profession. I had received Jesus, and I was willing to take any step that seemed appropriate. I was committed to following Jesus with all my heart. There was no area of my life that I knowingly withheld from His loving direction. I was baptized. I studied the Bible. I witnessed to my friends. But I did it all out of my love and passion for God. None of these things were done to earn anything from God. I knew that I had received everything I needed to live the life of my dreams.

Life in a denominational church may have been somewhat limiting, but it was not confusing. There was no emphasis on the promises of God for this life. In fact, the church really didn't believe that God did much other than provide the new birth.[2] They had only a vague concept of miracles. They viewed miracles as something that would happen only if God individually chose for them to happen.

---

2. This is in no way meant to minimize the value and gratitude I have for the new birth or for those people. If there were not another promise in this life, the new birth would be more than enough. However, there was much more.

I remember hearing the church people talk about how the age of miracles had passed away. I knew that could not be true. Without really seeking them, I had already experienced healing and miracles. I didn't know what to make of their limited view of God. As time passed I began to see that they were critical of people who seemed to experience more of God than they believed possible. It was at this point that I realized the need to move on.

*I knew that I had received everything
I needed to live the life of my dreams.*

My next move was into a church that would have been labeled as "charismatic." It was a good church in many respects. They believed in and prayed for miracles and healings. They did not limit God as much as the church I previously attended. But they presented an incredible list of qualifying conditions as prerequisites for receiving the promises of God. In other words, if you did not receive your miracle, then you should do a personal inventory to determine if you qualified. Although they offered the promises of God as a present reality, they connected a person to the sense of lack through their unscriptural eligibility requirements.

Even though all they said had a ring of truth, something did not quite fit. I got saved and didn't do anything to qualify. I got healed, and I didn't do anything to qualify for it. I was delivered from drugs, hatred, and violence and did nothing to qualify. As I looked at the New Testament examples of healing, I did not see Jesus or the early church apply the same rules for qualification that I was being presented at this church. This was the beginning of confusion for me.

It seemed that the groups who limited God to salvation had a good "doctrinal handle" on God's promises being free and fully paid for by Jesus' death, burial, and resurrection. As for the groups who believed that all the promises were for today, it seemed that they put forth more legalistic demands for qualification. It was as if they were saying, "Salvation is free; Jesus paid for that! But for everything else you must qualify by your personal merit." This need to qualify once again took the believer to the sense of lack. There was no consistent theological concept that governed this logic. It made God confusing and hard to understand.

After graduating from Bible College with a degree in theology, I began to check out many of the different groups. What I found was that almost all the groups believed the same things about God. Most groups believed that God would save you, heal you, and, yes, even work miracles. It seemed that what they disagreed on was the qualification factors. They all had different lists. They all insisted that their list was the true and accurate qualification for the promises of God. But regardless of the group or their list, followers ended up in legalism if they wanted to receive any of God's promises.

In each group good people who loved God and had good intentions struggled under lists that seemed as demanding as the list of the Pharisees. What I noticed as I talked to people from these different groups was that their lists did not make them feel closer to God. Their lists did not make them feel safe and loved. In fact, it was just the opposite; they felt afraid and isolated. It connected them to lack! Even when they were able to do the things on their lists, it did not endear them to God.

The Turning Point

This became a crucial factor for me when in 1978 I began a four-and-a-half year struggle with a kidney condition that could have cost me my life. After several operations, hospitalizations, and experimental drugs, I remained in a threatening medical state. I believed in healing, but I was not experiencing it. I was confused and afraid!

After a particular bout of sickness, weakness confined me to bed for a long period. Finally, I was strong enough to take a walk. I had been inside for weeks, and I just wanted to walk in the fresh air and pray. I wanted to breathe the life of the outdoors in my lungs. I wanted to feel alive. While walking and talking to God, I was acknowledging a scripture. I was saying, "Father, I thank You that I see You as You are and that I am being changed from glory to glory."[3]

Suddenly I heard that unmistakable voice of God in my heart. He said, "You don't see Me as I am." I became angry and argued with God. The third time He spoke to me He said, "In the area of healing you do not see Me as I am. You see Me as you have been led to believe I am." I repented on the very spot. I said, "Okay, if I don't see You as You are, I want to. I am willing to give up my view of You. Open my eyes. I want to see the truth!"

"You don't see Me as I am."

I went home, exhausted from the walk, and lay down for a nap. In a dream I saw every church service I had attended since being born again. It was like fanning through the pages of a book. In every service I saw the altar call. In each altar call what stood out to me was the stipulations that were placed on the promises of God. People who were seeking the much-needed promises of God were told what they had to do to qualify.

3.　Corinthians 3:18: *"But we all, with unveiled face, beholding as in a mirror the glory of the Lord, are being transformed into the same image from glory to glory, just as by the Spirit of the Lord."*

When I awoke I realized that I had subtly accepted all those stipulations. I had not done it willingly or by conscious choice. It was simply the product of repeated exposure. Repetition had reshaped my concept of God. I had lost the awareness that had been so real when I was first born again. I had forgotten that God had given me everything I ever needed completely independent of my personal qualifications. He had done it all because of His incredible love. And the one qualifying factor was the finished work of Jesus.

Repetition is a powerful tool. It is for that very reason God warns us, *"Cease, my son, to hear the instruction that causeth to err from the words of knowledge"* (Proverbs 19:27 KJV). Repetition has a way of making something seem real and true. We will believe a deception that we have always heard and reject truth that is obvious. It is a form of conditioning. We think because it is always said, it is true! Repetition makes what we hear permanent in our minds. It makes it real. And repetition of deception blinds us to God's reality!

That one law of personal development almost cost me my life. I had to restructure my beliefs. I had to find a way to write the truth on my heart so I could return to that simple place of relationship that I had once known. I had to release all the

We think because it is always said, it is true!

unscriptural stipulations I had placed on God. I had to decide if my trust was in the finished work of Jesus or in my personal performance. That decision was the beginning of freedom from a lifelong disease. It delivered me from the lack that religion had subtly reintroduced into my life.

Jesus is the one and only qualification for the promises of God! Jesus and His finished work must be the one and only object of our faith. *"For no matter how many promises God has made, they are 'Yes' in Christ"* (2 Corinthians 1:20 NIV). *"The Father who has qualified us to be partakers of the inheritance of the saints in the light"* (Colossians 1:12). If Jesus qualifies me for all the promises of God, why would I seek to be qualified again through my personal merit?

> *Jesus is the one and only*
> *qualification for the promises of God!*

As we build our lives around our lists, we slowly push Jesus from the center of our life. Our list may be good. It may contain things that we should do. The moment, however, that list becomes our qualification for God's approval, blessings, or acceptance, it has become our righteousness. We have rejected Jesus as our source of righteousness and qualification.

Each of us must make a clear and conscious decision about the source of our righteousness. Is our righteousness a gift from God, based on the finished work of Jesus, or is it based on our works? This decision is the starting place for breaking out of the up-and-down, in-and-out cycle. Consciously trusting Jesus as your righteousness will free you from the sense of lack and return you to a life filled with power and promise!

CHAPTER 7

WHAT WE WEREN'T TOLD

It has often been said that raising children would be easy if they came with an instruction manual. Then we wouldn't make all the mistakes inherent in parenting. Likewise, when we started our walk with God, we were like newborn babes. We didn't really know exactly what to do or how to do it. We needed someone to help us get off to a good start. We needed a manual!

The wonderful thing about starting out as a new believer is that we did get a manual. It is called the New Testament. When following the model laid out in those pages, a fabulous life is guaranteed. But, because it is not laid out in a simple format, we don't understand it. We need other people to help us get off to a good start.

The first few days of a new convert's life are crucial. During those first few days decisions are made that determine our paradigm of Christianity. It is in that time that our walk with God is usually determined. Those initial decisions often determine the rest of our life. Actually, it is these very early decisions that immediately drive us to a sense of lack or to a sense of wholeness.

When we came to Jesus, we should have started with a "clear plate." Someone should have told us to let go of everything we ever believed about God, to read the New Testament, and to start out fresh. Even the apostle Paul who was a scholar in the Old Testament realized that his understanding of God was not accurate. He needed to grow in his knowledge of God through the revelation of Jesus. After his conversion he spent fourteen years in preparation for his ministry. Before God could send him out to preach, he had to renew his mind in the principles of the New Covenant. His early attempts at ministry were a miserable failure that produced conflict and persecution.[1]

We tend to come to God laden with ideas and concepts from our past. Too many people never come to learn of God as He is. They bring a predetermined concept to their new life and say, "This is what I believe about God!" This is tantamount to what the children of Israel did when in their ignorance they created a golden calf and said, "This is the god who delivered us from Egypt!" The person who has a preconceived idea never gets to know God as He is. Starting from this corrupt logic makes it impossible to experience God as He is. The promise to see God is for the pure in heart, not the assumptive in heart.[2]

When I came to Jesus, a part of my prayer of salvation was, "Get me a Bible and I will read it. I will believe only what I find in the Bible. I will not believe what anyone says about You until I see it in the Bible." I had heard many strange things about God that I knew could not have possibly been true. I did not want what I had seen in other Christians. I had no interest in the fights I had seen over religious doctrine. I had no interest in a social gospel. I wanted what was real. I wanted to know God as He is!

Most Christians are willing to believe the truth. The problem is we get exposed to skewed concepts of the Scriptures and accept them as truth. Most of us have decided how we will see God before we have ever read the New Testament for

---

1. See Acts 9:28–31.
2. See Matthew 5:8.

the first time. Therefore, when we do read it, we simply notice the parts that reinforce our already corrupted beliefs.

Paul described the way we read the Bible as having a veil over our face. He said that the veil that blinds us and keeps us from seeing God as He really is, is the law. But he also says that when a person turns wholeheartedly to Jesus as Lord, that veil is removed and we are changed from glory to glory.[3] The problem, however, is that we think we are seeing God as He is when we really are seeing Him as He has been described to us.

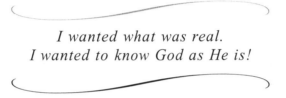

I wanted what was real.
I wanted to know God as He is!

The Bible says that wisdom is justified in her children.[4] In other words, all I have to do to determine if I am seeing God in truth is to look at the fruit. If I feel lack, insufficiency, or other negative emotions, if I have no hope, then I know that I am not committed to the truth. I may be fully committed to what I believe to be the truth, but if it does not have the power to set me free, then it is not truth. It is not according to God as revealed by the Lord Jesus Christ!

I may be fully committed to what I believe
to be the truth, but if it does not have
the power to set me free, then it is not truth.

Too often we mistakenly think that sincerity is evidence that we have believed the truth. When people challenge our

---

3.   See 2 Corinthians 3:13–18.

4.   See Luke 7:35 (KJV).

beliefs, we may feel they are challenging our sincerity. It is essential to realize that sincerity is not an indicator of our commitment to truth. It is, however, an indicator that once we get the truth we have the kind of attitude that will handle it with the care it deserves.

Many times in my walk with God I have had to take myself back to the bare realities and start over. When I realize, "I have been influenced by people more than the Bible," I repent and go back to the Word of God. I read it as if I had never read it before. I surrender my opinions and ego to the cross of Christ.

After the Lord showed me that I had developed a concept of His promises that was based on false stipulations, I re-read every verse and passage in the Bible about healing. I read it as if it was the first time. I renewed my mind in that area of my belief. Renewing my mind changed what I was experiencing. I have had to do that time and time again in other areas.

Jesus Is Our Righteousness

There were many things that we should have been told the day we were born again. So much of our struggle is not because we were told things that were wrong. It is because of what we were not told. We should have been saved for only a few minutes before someone shared the basics with us. Of all the things that we were not told, however, the most essential was that Jesus was our righteousness! He makes us whole and complete before God. Because of Him, we are qualified for all that God has and all that God is.

So much of our struggle is not because we were told things that were wrong. It is because of what we were not told.

Probably all who pray the prayer of salvation know they are accepting Jesus as their Savior. Some are fortunate enough to realize they are accepting Him as Lord. But nearly none knew they were accepting Him as their personal righteousness. I have asked thousands of people this simple question: "When you got saved, did anyone tell you that Jesus was going to be your righteousness?" Of the thousands around the world I have asked, less than ten were able to answer in the affirmative.

Without the realization that we are accepting Jesus as our righteousness, it is impossible for anything else to work as it should. Jesus as our righteousness is the matrix around which the entire Gospel "comes together." Without that as the core it becomes an unholy mixture of grace and law that paralyzes, blinds, and deceives the new convert. Without faith righteousness as the foundation, nothing ever really makes sense. The joys of salvation are mixed with apprehension and dread about the power to live the new life. The sense of lack then emerges from the inability to measure up as a Christian. We swap one torment for another!

Jesus as our righteousness is the matrix around which the entire Gospel "comes together."

Paul echoed the words of Jesus when he wrote to the Galatians and said, *"A little leaven leavens the whole lump"* (Galatians 5:9). These people had started out well. They wanted to know God. They accepted Jesus as Lord. But religious teachers seduced them. They taught the Galatians that Jesus would save them, but they had to obey the law to be righteous. As a result, the Galatians, like so many believers, unknowingly pushed Jesus out from the center of the Gospel.

These believers had good intentions, but the leaven of the law turned the Gospel into a damnable heresy that crippled instead of empowered. Without Jesus as their righteousness, it became impossible for them to experience the power and promises of God. The leaven Paul warned of was righteousness by works, or works righteousness.

Dead Works Don't Work

In Hebrews 6:1–2, Paul laid a foundation for New Testament faith. In these verses is the starting place for knowing God through the Lord Jesus. The very first of the foundational doctrines is *repentance from dead works*. The word *repent* as used in the New Testament simply means "a change of mind." In other words, when we come to God, we should change our mind about a lot of things, especially concerning the role that good works plays in our righteousness.

It is this very renewing of the mind that lies at the heart of making this journey with God. Your beliefs and ideas are like a map. They guide your every decision. You are living your life based on what you think works, what you think will get you what you want. You are following the map of your beliefs. In Christ, God's Word gives you a new map. As you expose your ideas and opinions to the Word of God, you can assess their validity. The Word of God becomes the new map that will guide your life; it becomes the new foundation upon which you build your life. If we as believers are not building on this foundation of faith righteousness, we will be limited to the best of our ability, or to our works.

When Paul recognized his need to repent, he was not talking about repentance from all the sinful things he was doing. He was talking about repentance from religious works. Paul was a very dedicated religious man. Everything he did was based on the Old Testament. It would have been easy for him to rationalize, since the Old and New Testaments talk about the same God, all of his views of God were accurate. Nothing could be farther from reality.

One of the things that the Old Testament never offered was righteousness. If the Israelites obeyed all of the law, it would be as if they were righteous. But it never actually made them righteous. *"And it shall be our righteousness, if we observe to do all these commandments before the Lord our God, as he hath commanded us"* (Deuteronomy 6:25 KJV). In Christ we are offered righteousness separate from our works.[5]

Complete and total obedience was as close to righteousness as the Old Testament believer would ever come. The truth is, however, that would never be enough to make a person acceptable to a holy, righteous God. David knew that his best efforts would never make him righteous. In Psalm 143:2 he prayed, *"Do not enter into judgment with Your servant, for in Your sight no one living is righteous."*

If obeying the law is a person's hope of righteousness, he would have to obey every single point. He could not fail at any part. If he did, he was not righteous enough to approach God. Paul cites a passage in Deuteronomy to make this point. *"All who rely on observing the law are under a curse, for it is written: 'Cursed is everyone who does not continue to do everything written in the Book of the Law' "* (Galatians 3:10 NIV).

The very law to which Paul had looked to see God actually hid God behind a veil. It allowed one to see a faint picture of God, but it never really showed Him as He is. *"But their minds were blinded. For until this day the same veil remains unlifted in the reading of the Old Testament, because the veil is taken away in Christ"* (2 Corinthians 3:14). God determined that people would see Him as He really is through the person of Jesus.

Paul had trusted in his obedience to the law to make him righteous. But he repented of all those "dead works." Granted,

---

5.   See Romans 4:6–8.

all the things he did for God were valuable. Many of them were things that he would continue to do, but he had to realize that none of those things could make him righteous—qualified and acceptable to God. That only happens because we are in Jesus.

Most of us came to God with predetermined ideas about who He was and what we would need to do to please Him. Because we held on to those ideas, we have alienated ourselves from the power of God. Therefore, we are stuck in the cycle of lack and destruction. We are connected to the sense of lack. We do as "good" as we can. Then one day we get tired, or angry, or frustrated. Then we don't do so "good." Immediately we lose our peace. We experience the only thing that law can give us; we experience the knowledge of sin, the sense of failure and lack. We believe that God is no longer close to us. We assume that He cannot possibly love us. We are now in the cycle of destruction. That destructive cycle will continue our entire life unless we follow Paul's example and repent of dead works.

Dead works are not the sinful things you do. That is sin. You need to repent of your sin. But your sin is the fruit of a deeper problem. It is the fruit of a life that is connected to the sense of lack, the absence of God's power. Dead works are those things you do to make yourself acceptable to God. It is those things that you trust to make you righteous more than you trust Jesus. No one may have ever told you this incredible truth. If you accepted Jesus as your Lord and Savior, then you are righteous through Him. There is not one thing you can do to make yourself more righteous.

When you accepted Jesus as Savior, did you accept Him as your righteousness? Did you connect to lack or to wholeness? Has life seemed harder since you got saved? Are you willing to accept Jesus as your righteousness now? If so, acknowledge Him right now as your righteousness. Every time

*If you accepted Jesus as your Lord and Savior,
then you are righteous through Him. There is not
one thing you can do to make yourself more righteous.*

you begin to feel lack, remind yourself that Jesus has made
you righteous before God. As you do so, with each passing
day this reality will grow in your heart and empower you to
new heights of freedom and joy!

CHAPTER 8

THE HEART OF THE GOSPEL

Without the realization of faith righteousness and grace, the New Testament seems to be little more than an addendum of the Old. The New Testament is not a part of the Old Testament, however. It is a completely new arrangement between God and man. It comes with better promises, better terms, and more power. It is good news!

The word *gospel* literally means "good news." Some Bible translations call it the "Great News"! Jesus brought us the Gospel. He brought us news from God that was so much better than anything people had ever heard that it was called the good news. It must have been hard to imagine what could possibly be better than anything God had ever said or done up to that point.

In John 1:17 we get our first glimpse of this incredibly great news. *"For the law was given through Moses, but grace and truth came through Jesus Christ."* Moses gave us the law, and it was completely true. But the law had several weaknesses. The first and most significant weakness of the law was that it could never make a person righteous. Therefore, the participants could never have a sense of wholeness. Hebrews 10:1 says it this way: *"For the law having a shadow of good things to come, and not the very image of the things, can never with those sacrifices which they offered year by year continually make the comers thereunto perfect"* (KJV).

The Law Could Do Only So Much

Although the law had incredible value, it did not have the power to transform. It merely gave rules whereby one could live a more peaceful and productive life. The law provided the most sophisticated, comprehensive social codes available to man. It taught man such things as how to eat and how to have a judicial system that worked. It provided principles for health, a financial system, and more. Also built into the law were principles that would prepare man for the ultimate revelation of God. The sacrificial system was the "shadow" through which man could get a glimpse of the coming Lord and Savior. But not one person was ever set free by the law!

Although the law provided all of these valuable systems, it was full of inherent weaknesses—the biggest problem being that it had no power to transform anyone. The law never gave a person a clear conscience. It never delivered people from the internal sense of lack. It never gave mankind the power to break free from the endless cycle of commitment, effort, and ultimate failure. It could only offer a model of behavioral modification. It could tell you what to do, but offer you no power or help to do it. So it was a perfect standard offered to imperfect men who could never live up to its standard. Imagine how disheartening that had to be!

Because it was being applied to men who had not been transformed, it was impossible for them to obey from the heart. *"For what the law could not do in that it was weak through the flesh, God did by sending His own Son..."* (Romans 8:3). What God wanted to accomplish in mankind could never be done externally. Nor could it ever be done by man's efforts. The law simply provided a system of guidelines for man to live until God's ultimate intention could be made a reality.

Because man failed at obeying the law, it created another weakness. It made man sin-conscious. *"Therefore by the deeds of the law there shall no flesh be justified in his sight: for by the law is the knowledge of sin"* (Romans 3:20 KJV). Nothing could be more emotionally destructive than seeking to serve a holy God with a continual awareness of all the areas in which you had failed. Sin consciousness, contrary to the beliefs of some, does not make you live a better life. In fact, it makes you live a worse life. It binds the practitioner to an abiding sense of lack. You are constantly made aware of your limitations and inabilities.

The law simply provided a system of guidelines for man to live until God's ultimate intention could be made a reality.

Paul said in 1 Corinthians 15:56 that *"the strength of sin is the law"* (KJV). How could this be? The very law that God gave to show man how to live a peaceful, productive life ultimately caused man to get worse. So was the law bad? No! The problem was the heart of mankind. Man, who had a sin nature and a sense of failure, became more corrupt and hypocritical. Law was a destructive thing for unregenerate men. God could only solve the problem in Jesus. What the law could not do, Jesus did!

So Moses gave the law, but Jesus gave *"grace and truth."* The law had no power to make people better. It was just a list of rules that, when followed, would make life better. But it was dependent on sinful men to work. A complete impossibility!

Grace and Truth Did What the Law Could Not

Jesus, on the other hand, not only brought truth, but He also brought a higher level of truth. What Jesus called upon man to do far exceeded what the law had required. Jesus not only taught us to walk in the truth, He also taught us to do it from a heart that was motivated by love—love for God and love for people. He didn't "lower the bar"; He raised it to a level of impossibility for men with a sin nature.

Fortunately, Jesus did not just bring a new level of truth; He brought grace as well! Grace is more than unmerited favor. Grace is God's power, ability, and capacity that works in a person's heart and is given without merit.[1] Grace is God's ability that works in man. It is God's power that makes us able to do what we could not possibly do in our own limited ability. The Old Testament gave us rules filled with wisdom, but it did not empower us to obey those rules. Jesus came to raise the standards for all those rules. They had to work from the heart, from the motive of love. But He did not leave us to our own limitations. He gave us the power and capacity to live that truth.

How would God give us this power? What form would it take? The power that God gives us, the power that makes us able to live in His Word, is the power of righteousness. When trying to discuss righteousness with people, I have found that few can actually connect with a literal definition. It is not, however, the definition of righteousness that empowers us to break free from the destructive cycle of lack. The key to righteousness empowering us is in how it affects self-awareness, or in how we feel. To feel righteous is to feel complete and whole. It is to feel clean and acceptable before God. It is to have an absolute sense of qualification, an absolute knowing about God's acceptance and provision in every area of life. It is this sense of empowerment that gives us the confidence to trust God and yield to righteousness.

God has given us a new, righteous nature. He has made us a completely new creation. This is the great news! This is the most significant thing God has done for mankind since creation. He sent Jesus to become a man, live a sinless life, go to a cross, become our sin, take our punishment, die for our sins, obtain righteousness, be raised from the dead, and offer

---

1.   Joseph Henry Thayer, *Thayer's Greek English Lexicon of the New Testament* (Grand Rapids, Michigan: Baker Book House, 1977).

it to us as a free gift. Second Corinthians 5:21 says it this way: *"For He made Him who knew no sin to be sin for us, that we might become the righteousness of God in Him."*

The power that God gives us, the power that makes us able to live in His Word, is the power of righteousness.

When we are born again, we actually become a new creation. Yes, we are the same individual. We have all of our life's memories and experiences. But we are given a new nature. We are given a righteous nature. This new nature empowers us to live a new life. We now have a new capacity and ability to live in a manner pleasing to God and to our own conscience. We are freed from the sense and power of lack.

Experiencing the greatest news God has ever given to mankind should be an incredibly exuberant experience. If in fact we have believed this incredible news about faith righteousness, if we are experiencing the sense of wholeness, then our life should be dominated by that reality. It should affect the way we approach everything in our life.

As a believer I have to ask myself, does my relationship with Jesus bring a positive effect into every area of my life? If not, what is it I believe about God and me? Do I feel clean and whole before God? Do I feel empowered to live the life to which God has called us? Do I feel like the Gospel is the best news I have ever heard? How I answer these questions is an indication of whether or not I have really believed the Great News about Jesus.

There is a simple self-test you can apply to recognize how you really feel about anything. Look in the mirror. Look straight into your eyes and say, "You are completely righteous." Now wait to see what emotions and thoughts emerge in response to this statement. Write them down. These thoughts, emotions, and reactions represent the underlying feelings you have about your righteousness. Once you recognize these feelings, you can begin to make changes about your acceptance of the great news that Jesus is your righteousness.

Go back to the mirror and say to your reflection, "Jesus has made you righteous. You are completely acceptable to God. He finds no fault in you. You stand before Him holy and blameless in love." Use our *Prayer Organizer*[2] to make yourself aware of the hundreds of scriptures that proclaim your new righteous identity in Jesus. Acknowledge who you are in Christ until you reach a place where you feel complete peace and joy when you say it. Make it your reality, and it will become your power.

---

2.   You can obtain *The Prayer Organizer* from Impact International Publications, 3516 S. Broad Place, Huntsville, AL 35805. Or log on to www. impactministries.com.

CHAPTER 9

FROM FIRST TO LAST

"I just can't get this to work," he sighed. "I've got victory in other areas, but this is just too strong. No matter how hard I try, nothing changes." This was certainly not the first time I had heard this story. Like so many Christians, Terry was caught in the cycle. Even though God had given him victory in other areas, he was about to "throw in the towel" over this seemingly insurmountable issue. Of course, it was a significant issue!

"Maybe you're asking the wrong question," I suggested.

"What are you talking about?" came the somewhat angry reply.

"You keep asking what you need to *do* to get victory over this problem, but maybe you need to be asking 'What do I need to *believe*?' " I suggested.

"What are you talking about? I am a believer," Terry insisted.

"Yes, you're a believer. You believe on Jesus to get you to heaven. But what do you believe Jesus can do about this problem?"

"Why should He do anything? He's not going to answer my prayers when I am stuck in sin like this!" was the sharp comeback.

"At the root of every problem is what you believe," I insisted. "Do you believe you are righteous in Jesus?"

"How could you ask me that?" he blurted. "You know how I have struggled with this issue. No! I'm not righteous. I want to be, but I can't overcome this sin."

Like many Christians, Terry thought his righteousness was defined by his actions. He couldn't see beyond his works. He wanted his works to make him righteous. He was caught in the cycle. He believed Jesus gave him enough righteousness to get him born again but not enough righteousness to conquer his sin. Instead of trusting in the power of righteousness to deliver him from sin, he trusted in his works to earn his righteousness. He had no consistency in his belief of the Gospel. Without a change in his beliefs, he would spend he rest of his life in the cycle of lack.

Inconsistency in the Gospel seems to be interwoven in every great theological challenge facing the church—especially in the area of faith righteousness! Faith righteousness is the theological foundation of the New Testament. Every doctrine should be built on this reality. Yet, the church has wrestled with this foundational truth since its inception. Nearly every epistle was written to bring believers back to a place of trusting Jesus as their righteousness. Somehow, though, we have missed that message. There seems to be some vague concept of Jesus qualifying us for salvation. But we somehow fail to see Him as qualifying us for anything else.

Nearly every epistle was written to bring believers back to a place of trusting Jesus as their righteousness.

A Radical Message

Paul's message turned the world upside down. Nothing so radical had ever before been heard. Every kind of god and every kind of doctrine had been preached to the Roman world.

But nothing like this! Now, the idea of a savior was not that different. Belief in deities was common. But every concept of religion had placed the burden of satisfying the gods on the shoulders of the believer. Man was enslaved to serving and satisfying the angry, moody gods. Man existed in a continual state of need, always seeking the undeserved favor of an angry god.

The idea that righteousness could be a free gift was beyond comprehension. This far-reaching idea is in fact the source of both incredible persecution from those who did not believe and inconceivable power for those who did believe. *"For I am not ashamed of the gospel of Christ, for it is the power of God to salvation for everyone who believes"* (Romans 1:16). It is the sense of wholeness that comes through faith righteousness that breaks the crippling grip of religion and sets a person free to know the living God.

The Gospel is designed to bring power and wholeness into the life of every believer. Connection with Almighty God should free us from the connection to lack. The power of righteousness should break the grip of sin. The power of life should overcome every shadow of death that works in our lives. We should be affected at every level of our existence with the power of righteousness. We should have a new sense of identity that infuses our sense of self. This is not a description of the exceptional Christian life. This is the model for the normal Christian life.

Paul insisted that there was a connection between experiencing this power and maintaining consistency in faith righteousness. Paul's bold statement, *"I am not ashamed of the gospel,"* calls forth memories of the times we may not have shared the message of Jesus or times we were intimidated and did not stand up for Jesus. However, being a bold witness is not the main point being made. He was making a specific reference to the good news about Jesus being our source of righteousness.

Verse 17 continues, *"For in it* [the gospel] *the righteousness of God is revealed from faith to faith."*

It was not the idea that Jesus was Savior that made the Gospel message so radical. Many of the people who persecuted Paul believed that Jesus was Savior. The thing that was so radical was the inconceivable idea that Jesus was our righteousness. This idea, which is the very core of the Gospel, has always been more than the natural mind could grasp.

The thing that was so radical was the inconceivable idea that Jesus was our righteousness.

Religion functions in lack. It holds men captive to its gods through lack, not love. Religious dedication and subsequent commitment is based on fear, control, and self-righteousness. The idea of righteousness by faith is the part of the Gospel with which Christians struggle. Paul identified this belief as the stumbling stone of the Gospel.[1] Yet, amazingly, it is the heart of the Gospel. The entire Gospel is built upon this foundation. Apart from faith righteousness, the Gospel is no more appealing and offers no more hope than any other religion.

It is the failure to embrace Jesus as our righteousness that keeps us bound to the sense of lack. It keeps us repeating the

Apart from faith righteousness, the Gospel is no more appealing and offers no more hope than any other religion.

destructive cycle of failure, shame, frustration, and recommitment. When we are not experiencing the power of God, the issue of faith righteousness is always at the root. The areas of

---

1.   See Romans 9:32–33.

our life that do not work are the areas in which we don't connect our beliefs to faith righteousness.

The Cornerstone for Our Belief

We have not actually believed the Gospel until we have believed that Jesus is our righteousness. This is what must be believed in order for the Gospel to have power in our lives. The message of faith righteousness facilitates the power that frees us from the sense of lack and ends the cycle of the struggle to please, which results in failure and defeat.

From first to last, every aspect of our walk with God is dependent upon our belief in the righteousness of Jesus as our own. For example, when we need peace, we have to ask ourselves, "Did Jesus obtain peace through His death, burial, and resurrection? Does being in Jesus qualify me for that peace?" These are the only two questions I need answered when facing any of life's obstacles: Did Jesus obtain the promised solution? Does being in Him qualify me?

Herein lies the solution to the righteousness issue. Do you believe the righteousness of Jesus is enough to qualify you for all the promises of God? Until that issue is resolved, you have no foundation upon which to build the promises of the New Covenant. Until the righteousness of Jesus is your qualification, you will attempt to overcome the sense of lack through your own sacrifices and good deeds. Thus you are bound to the repetitive cycle of destruction. By seeking your own righteousness, you have rejected His righteousness and the power it brings.

Our logic cannot seem to grasp the concept of faith righteousness. It is as if we can believe that Jesus gave us enough righteousness to get born again, but we are not sure if He gave us enough righteousness to qualify for anything else. Our "works mentality" dominates our faith in the finished work of Jesus. It neutralizes the power of righteousness in our life. We are limited to the best we can do instead of resting in the best He could do.

We have turned the entire doctrine of righteousness upside down. We think that if we do good enough we will qualify for the promises of God. The truth is if you could do good enough you would not need the promises of God. They would no longer be promises; rather, they would be wages. God did not save us from sin and then leave us on our own. He came to live in us. He abides in us. His righteous nature is in us by the Holy Spirit.

Romans 1:17 says, *"For in it the righteousness of God is revealed from faith to faith; as it is written, 'The just shall live by faith."* There is no part of the Christian walk from the first to the last and everything in between that is not based on faith...faith in the righteousness of Jesus as our own.

Do something every day to remind yourself that Jesus is your righteousness. Begin each day acknowledging who you are in Jesus. Let that be the mind-set that sets your course. When you lie down to sleep, take the last few minutes before falling off to sleep and remind yourself that Jesus is your righteousness. Very soon your sense of self will be swallowed up in His righteousness. That sense of righteousness will drive away the sense of lack!

CHAPTER 10

THE POWER OF RIGHTEOUSNESS

The concept of faith righteousness is a paradox. It seems so contradictory. Those who do not understand it think that it is a form of "easy believism." Some falsely think that faith righteousness leads to a compromised life. Nothing could be farther from the truth. Accepting the righteousness of Jesus as our own connects us to the power of righteousness. Faith righteousness gives us the only escape from the sense of lack that draws us into sin.

In the previous chapter I told how Terry felt that his compromised lifestyle meant he was not righteous. He felt that if he would only live right, that would make him righteous, thereby qualifying him for the promises of God. He felt that God would not help him because he was so undeserving. Terry was trapped in the cycle of lack.

The mental maze of works righteousness is an illogical enigma. It connects you to the sense of lack. It buries you in an endless cycle that allows you to momentarily come up for

The mental maze of works righteousness is an illogical enigma.

breath before plunging you once again beneath the torrents of negative emotions. Like the plight of a swimmer caught in white-water rapids, it is an endless, frightening struggle for life. Just when you think you can take a breath, it plunges you down into the frightening abyss of toiling in fear and darkness. No matter how hard one may try, righteousness by works never delivers what it promises!

The Law—A Substitute for the Promise

Righteousness is the one thing man did not possess under the Old Covenant. The law did not make people righteous. It was, in fact, a substitute for righteousness. It was a list of procedures that displayed the wisdom of God. It revealed what a righteous person would do. Obeying the law was tantamount to imitating righteousness. But it did not make them righteous.

In Deuteronomy 6:1 God said, *"Now this is the commandment, and these are the statutes and judgments which the Lord your God has commanded to teach you, that you may observe them in the land which you are crossing over to possess."* The law was given for their good. God was showing the Israelites how to function in an antagonistic land and remain victorious. It was a formula for success in a hostile world.

In verse 6 God emphasized the importance of this instruction. *"And these words which I command you today shall be in your heart."* The law was essential to the survival of Israel. It was a means whereby unregenerated man could experience the blessings of a holy God. He wanted these words to be a part of their internal belief system, thereby guiding them through life. But God never wanted His people to think that these laws would make them righteous.

In verse 25 of this same passage we see the flawed logic of the children of Israel when they said, *"And it shall be our righteousness, if we observe to do all these commandments"* (KJV). God never said the law could make you righteous. In fact, He said just the opposite. *"No man is justified by the law in the sight of God, it is evident: for, The just shall live by faith"* (Galatians 3:11 KJV).

Like the children of Israel, we trust more in our perform-ance for righteousness than in God's promise of righteousness in Jesus. Works righteousness just makes sense when you look

God never said the law could make you righteous. In fact, He said just the opposite.

at it in a natural way. This is what Paul was talking about in Romans 8:7 when he said, *"The carnal mind is enmity against God: for it is not subject to the law of God, neither indeed can be."* Even though it makes sense, it separates you from the ability to live in the righteousness of God. It opposes all that God did through the death, burial, and resurrection of Jesus. It actual-ly disempowers you and sets the stage for your ultimate de-mise. Yet, it makes sense!

The Power Is in the Promise

God defied all logic when He introduced the idea of righ-teousness apart from works. *"But now the righteousness of God apart from the law is revealed, being witnessed by the Law and the Prophets, even the righteousness of God, through faith in Jesus Christ, to all and on all who believe"* (Romans 3:21–22). The church has resisted the possibility of this promise ever since Jesus ascended into heaven. We have stubbornly clung to the concept of works righteousness even though it has never pro-duced a church or an individual who had the power to change the world.

Under the law, man did not have an internal sense of righteousness. Under the New Covenant, however, we have been given a new nature. We are a new creation. We have been made righteous. The new birth is a birth into righteousness. We should do whatever it takes to connect with the sense of righteousness. It is that sense of righteousness that keeps us connected to the power of righteousness.

Righteousness is more than a right standing with God. It is more than an imputed status. It is more than a theological concept. Righteousness is also the power of God to live in

We should do whatever it takes
to connect with the sense of righteousness.

righteousness. It is the strength that comes into us as a result of receiving this new nature. It is ever present. It abides in us through the person of the Holy Spirit, who lives in us. It is our right standing and it is our power to stand right. It makes us feel right about ourselves and God. And it gives us the power to live right before God.

When we fall into sin, it is usually in an attempt to pacify our sense of lack. But, instead of quenching the longing, it breeds new levels of insecurity and desperation. It convinces us that we are not in fact righteous. Any attempt to "get right with God" is an effort in work righteousness. Any attempt to get right with God reinforces the idea that we are not, in fact, right with God. It is an alienation from the power of righteousness that is in us as we pursue a righteousness of our own.

So here we find ourselves deep in the cycle. We are struggling with a sin that makes us feel unrighteous. We have lost our confidence with God. We felt that if we could only live a better life, we would feel righteous again and all of our confidence would return. Then we could believe that we are accepted of God.

The problem is that we don't have the power to consistently conquer the sin to which we feel drawn. Even when we stop committing the action, we still struggle with the desire, the temptation. Our vulnerability makes us feel weak, inadequate…lacking!

See if you can grasp the contradictory logic: My sin makes me feel unrighteous. I need righteousness, which I do not have, to have the power to overcome my sin. So I seek to become righteous in my own strength in order to gain righteousness. Then I no longer need God's righteousness…. The logic and the outcome are bizarre.

Because we have been born again, we have the righteousness of God inside us. We did not have the inherent power of righteousness in our sinful nature. And according to the epistle to the Romans, we were slaves to a sinful nature. So we didn't have a choice. Now we do. We don't have to yield to sin; we can choose to yield to righteousness. And whatever we yield to, empowers our life.

The idea of yielding is foreign to Western Christianity. We have been trained to make things happen—to become righteous by doing righteous. However, if the power of righteousness is in me, then I don't need to *become* righteous; I need to *yield to* the power of righteousness. As a believer I now have options. Sin may compel me, but it has no power over me until I decide to yield to it. Then its power goes to work in me to make me a slave to sin.

Simultaneously, even though sin is compelling me, righteousness is in me. The desire to sin may have caused me to lose my sense of righteousness, but righteousness has not left me. Rather, I am connecting to sin as I meditate on it. As I entertain the pleasure it will bring, sin becomes more real and alive in me than righteousness. Sin is not my master; it is simply the thing to which I am emotionally connecting through my thoughts.

I can do the same thing with righteousness that I do with sin. I can begin to think about the joys of walking with God. I can remind myself that I am righteous in Jesus. As I magnify righteousness and its joys above sin, I reconnect to righteousness. As I once again sense its presence, I can yield to its power.

There are times when we may not yield to righteousness, but that does not mean we are not righteous. Paul did not tell us to become righteous in order to conquer our sin problems.

We don't have to yield to sin;
we can choose to yield to righteousness.

He told us to yield to righteousness. *"Yield yourselves unto God, as those that are alive from the dead, and your members as instruments of righteousness unto God"* (Romans 6:13 KJV). It is not about becoming; it is about yielding.

The more we establish a righteousness consciousness or an awareness of Jesus' righteousness in us, the more we are likely to yield to it. Consciousness determines connection. That which is present in our awareness is that to which we are connected. The more the reality of righteousness permeates our sense of self, the more we experience it as an emotional reality that dominates and empowers all our decisions.

In every temptation, remind yourself that you are righteous. Thank God that Jesus is in you and that you are alive to His righteousness. Experience the complete victory over sin as you yield to the power of righteousness. Join the millions who trust in His righteousness and live in victory! The power is in you. You don't need anyone to bring it to you; just yield.

CHAPTER 11

FLAWED LOGIC

Our flawed religious logic keeps us connected to the sense of lack, thereby trapping us in an endless cycle of destruction. How does it work? First we create beliefs based on our experiences. That subjective illusion becomes our sense of reality. Then we create a theology that explains the lie. The whole thing is what I call circumstance theology.[1]

Hebrews 11:3 explains God's process for believing that leads to understanding. *"By faith we understand that the worlds were framed by the word of God, so that the things which are seen were not made of things which are visible."* The way our mind comes to understand God's phenomenon starts with believing. Once we believe, our mind gains the capacity to perceive and understand.

What we are not willing to believe, we will never have the capacity to receive. You see, our mind works to prove that which we choose to believe. There is no such thing as a totally unbiased thought. We all are guided by our preconceived ideas. A person must at least be open to a possibility before he or she can see and perceive that possibility.

In the book, *Show Me God*, Fred Heeren and George Smoot record the intellectual pursuits of some of the greatest minds of the past century who did not believe there was a God. They

---

1. For more information on this topic, see my book, *Taking the Limits Off God*, available from Impact International Publications, 3516 S. Broad Place, Huntsville, AL, 35805, or by logging on to www.impact ministries.com.

set out on an intellectual quest to prove or disprove the existence of God. In the end they reached the undeniable conclusion that the world had to be created by an intelligent being—that is, God. What is significant, however, is that the unique characteristic that made these people such intellectual greats was their openness to any possibility. This subtle but essential factor meant they were open to all possibilities. If there are any possibilities to which we are not open, then we can never discover the truth about them because our mind cannot reveal what we will not see. The Bible says it this way: *"The pure in heart...shall see God"* (Matthew 5:8).

When I was first saved—when I first acknowledged Jesus as my Savior—I knew nothing about God. Fortunately I was

If there are any possibilities to which we are not open,
then we can never discover the truth about them
because our mind cannot reveal what we will not see.

aware of my ignorance. In my prayer of salvation I acknowledged, "God, get me a Bible. I will read it and believe it. I will believe about You only what I can see in the Bible for myself." As I read through the Bible, I would come upon things that I didn't know or didn't believe. When that happened, I would simply fall to my knees and pray, "God, I don't know what this means, but I am willing to believe it. Will You help me to see and understand it?" The willingness to accept what I didn't know or understand protected me against flawed logic.

When we start from a place of trust, the Spirit of God can take us down the path of understanding. An open mind gives Him the freedom to fulfill His role as the great teacher. Our problem is we want to understand before we are willing to trust. We want God to explain an infinite reality in a way that our finite mind can grasp. Instead of having the attitude of a disciple, we sit in the seat of the scorner. We want God to submit His wisdom to our judgment. In our smug self-righteousness, we approve or disapprove of God's wisdom based on our limited understanding. The result is we do not allow God to take us to any level of existence that we do not understand.

When we insist that we must understand before we trust, we turn the entire process upside down. Belief that is based on understanding is subject to change if someone else comes

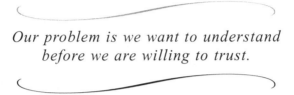

*Our problem is we want to understand
before we are willing to trust.*

along and presents a stronger or more reasonable argument. When our logic is the reasoning that directs our beliefs, we are like a boat tossed by the waves of the circumstance.

The Results Reveal the Logic

According to John 1:1, Jesus was the *logos* of God. The *logos* is the integrity, wisdom, and logic behind the Word. All of God's words are upheld by a wisdom and logic that is revealed in the person of Jesus. *"Who being the brightness of his glory, and the express image of his person, and upholding all things by the word of his power"* (Hebrews 1:3 KJV). We should be able to observe the life of Jesus and grasp the logic of God. His life should give us our basis of understanding how God relates to mankind. When our reasoning becomes the center of the equation, we make ourselves to be the *logos* of God. Then we really believe God is revealed and understood in our reasoning.

From these vain imaginations we create a concept of God that fits into our logic. It is the purest form of idolatry. We have created an image of God independent of how He reveled Himself through Jesus. We build entire religious systems around the empty theories that emerge from our corrupt logic. We gather people around us and persuade them that our position is correct. We are like the Pharisees Jesus addressed: *"Woe to you, teachers of the law and Pharisees, you hypocrites! You travel over land and sea to win a single convert, and when he becomes one, you make him twice as much a son of hell as you are"* (Matthew 23:15 NIV). We want everyone to believe what we believe whether it helps people or not. The more we get others to agree with our logic, the more we are falsely assured that ours are the thoughts of God.

Then we commit our lives to protecting these ideas. Over the centuries men have excluded and rejected those who disagree with their doctrines. Laws have been passed to make it illegal to believe anything that differs from a particular point of view. People have been tormented and murdered to preserve doctrine. All this violence was generated in an attempt to protect the illusionary concepts of God that we all have agreed to call reality. The need to violently defend our beliefs is the greatest sign that those beliefs have not empowered our life. Instead, they are simply the dogma to which we look for security.

If these doctrines were based on the *logos* of God, they would produce the same fruit in our lives that Jesus presented in His life. They would heal and deliver. They would breed value and worth for all people. They would make us more kind and patient. Love would be the motive and goal of all our actions. New Testament beliefs make us become more like Jesus.

All our attempts to violently preserve our doctrines emerge from the sense of lack. Every seed bears after its own kind.[2] Bad seed produces bad fruit. Good seed produces good fruit. Lack and fear always are present at the same time. One always gives rise to the other. They are a continuum of unscriptural beliefs, emotions, and consequences. We should

---

2.   See Genesis 1:12.

never allow a belief that makes us feel threatened to drive our actions. Acting on a negative belief is like planting handfuls of thorn bush seeds in the garden of our life. They create snares and pain that keep us from the life Jesus died to give us.

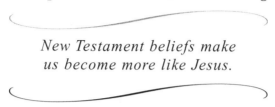

New Testament beliefs make us become more like Jesus.

God desires to take us to a quality of life that is beyond our comprehension. First Corinthians 2:9 tells us, *"Eye has not seen, nor ear heard, nor have entered into the heart of man the things which God has prepared for those who love Him."* In our attempt to fit God into our flawed logic, we have limited our experience with God to our subjective reasoning. Consequently, we have come to believe in God as He exists in our mind, and that image may be a total contradiction to what Jesus showed us.

Psalm 78:41 says, about the children of Israel, *"Again and again they tempted God."* The children of Israel continually judged God. They would hear His promise and then they would pass a judgment as to whether they believed He was able to fulfill that promise. The second half of that same verse in Psalm 78 tells us they *"limited the Holy One of Israel."* Our judgments of God limit His ability to express Himself in our life. That limited expression then becomes the deceitful proof that our flawed logic is correct. It is a trap from which there is no deliverance apart from repentance.

The hardships of the children of Israel were not the cruel testing of God. His only test for them was the test of believing. He offered them promises, and their faith was tested with every promise. Did they believe or not believe the promise? When they believed the promise, their faith passed the test and they experienced the promise. When they doubted the promise, they limited their experience with God and became subject to their circumstances, which were often quite destructive.

As Paul said in First Corinthians, God is always tying to take us to a place we have never seen with our eyes nor conceived in our heart. He would have us take wings and rise above the lack that abounds in a world dominated by the curse of man's logic.

How could we possibly rise above our current perspective of life? Psalm 78:42 helps us understand the downfall of the people of Israel. *"They did not remember His power: the day when He redeemed them from the enemy."* The disciples fell into the same trap when they thought they would die in the storm. When faced with impossible circumstances, they didn't consider the miracles they had seen Jesus work. They let their mind be taken captive by their fearful emotions.[3] They limited God's ability to deliver to the scope of their fears.

God included His mighty works in the Bible so we would have a record of His deeds to give us courage when we face trouble. In Jesus we are qualified to receive any promise that God ever made to anyone in the Bible.[4] He will do for us what He has done for anyone. Our sense of lack, though, tells us that we are disqualified. Our rejection of righteousness in Jesus makes our unbelief become a self-fulfilling prophecy that confirms our delusion.

The Spirit of God is always trying to lead us into all the possibilities of God. Although our eyes have not seen it, Paul assured us in 1 Corinthians 2:10, *"But God has revealed them to us through His Spirit. For the Spirit searches all things, yes, the deep things of God."* God is trying to show us what our eyes have never seen. He is seeking to reveal what has never entered into our heart. He wants to take us where we don't know how to go. He wants to remove the limits of our reasoning.

---

3.   See Mark 6:52.

4.   See 2 Corinthians 1:20.

When the sense of righteousness permeates your heart, you will be free from the fear that binds you to lack and open your heart to all the possibilities of God. Start by accepting God's reality of righteousness. Believe that you are qualified in Jesus, and open your heart and mind to all the possibilities of all His promises.

In Jesus we are qualified to receive any promise that God ever made to anyone in the Bible.

Free yourself from flawed logic by putting Jesus back at the center of your equation. Open your heart to God by praying this simple prayer: "Father, I want to know You through Jesus. I want to see You as You are. I will not limit You to my understanding or past experiences. As I read the Word, help me to see You as You really are." Now read the Gospels, and when you see Jesus handle a problem or reach out to someone, remind yourself that He is showing you God. Bring all of your flawed ideas about God in line with the life of Jesus. When you find something you don't understand, don't assume you know what it means. Instead, entrust yourself to the Holy Spirit as the great teacher. Simply surrender your ideas and await His wisdom. It will come!

CHAPTER 12

TRAPPED BY MY OPINION

Humility is the mind-set that facilitates the manifestation of incredible aspects of God. *"Humble yourselves in the sight of the Lord, and he shall lift you up"* (James 4:10 KJV). Unfortunately, our religious concepts of humility place "great things" and "humility" at opposite ends of the spectrum. Yet, according to God's Word, the two depend on one another.

Humility is not a position of degradation and defeat. It is actually a place of great confidence. The humble person recognizes the limitations of his finite mind without feeling lack or inadequacy. Such people are completely at peace with the wisdom of surrendering personal opinions to God's, thereby submitting their will to God's will. Their trust in God makes surrender a safe, positive experience. They trust God's will for their lives. They know that God alone can bring them to the place of absolute fulfillment.

The haughty and the proud, however, cling tenaciously to their opinions regardless of God's opinion. They falsely believe that they will not experience the best if they surrender to God. They do not understand that as our shepherd, God leads us away from lack and into His best. This blindness plunges people into the cycle of lack and defeat. No matter how many times they repeat the cycle, they fail to realize that their vain imagination and proud heart are at the root of the problem.

It's All About Opinion

Jesus told the Pharisees that they remained in blindness because they insisted that they could see. *"Jesus said to them, 'If you were blind, you would have no sin; but now you say, "We see." Therefore your sin remains' "* (John 9:41). Few things have the power to blind us more than our own opinions. Our proud insistence that we see things as they are, keeps us limited to the power of our perception.

It is our opinions and our subsequent actions based on those opinions that lead us deeper and deeper into destructive cycles. Until our opinion changes, we will repeat all our past failures because all of our decisions are based on our flawed logic. Proverbs 16:25 says it like this: *"There is a way that seems*

*Few things have the power
to blind us more than our own opinions.*

right to a man, but in the end it leads to death" (NIV). This is why God calls us to repentance. Repentance does not qualify us for the promises. Rather, repentance facilitates our ability to see what we have never before seen! Repentance opens our heart to new options and new understanding.

The word *repent* simply means "a change of mind," or to think differently. In order for us to see what we need to see, we have to be freed from the limited opinions that shape our perception. It is our opinions that we must surrender. Even when we do not know what the proper belief or point of view should be, we should always live in a mind-set that is ready to surrender our opinion to God's opinion.

At first glance this seems as if it would breed instability. After all, if we are committed to what we believe, how could we easily surrender it to a new thought or idea? In the paradox of life we must find that place where we are fully committed to our beliefs but ready to surrender them to the view and opinion of God. This can happen only when Jesus Himself is our source of safety. The humble heart is fully committed to God and His Word yet fully flexible in adjusting its understanding of that Word.

Too often our doctrine serves as a wall to isolate us from God instead of a bridge to lead us to God. Doctrine produces dogma; relationship produces stability. When our confidence is in our doctrine, we have a sense of safety only when our doctrine is protected. When our sense of well-being emerges from our relationship with Jesus, our doctrine can be challenged without it affecting our sense of wholeness.

In the Old Testament, millions of people sought to relate to God on the basis of the law. But the people who were immortalized as those *"of whom the world was not worthy"*[1] were those who lived by faith. Their trust was not in the law or the false sense of righteousness it could bring. Their trust was in a relationship with God. They sought to obey the law. They knew it was the wisdom of God. But they trusted God personally for their sense of security.

Too often our doctrine serves as a wall to isolate us from God instead of a bridge to lead us to God.

Shortly after being born again, I received a call from a family member who said, "I appreciate the change in your behavior, but you're still going to hell." This person's hope of salvation was in her denomination. She insisted that salvation was the result of attending a particular church. I have to admit

---

1.   Hebrews 11:38.

that I was momentarily shaken. But I also was more than willing to subject my beliefs to her scrutiny. In the midst of the challenge I felt safe with God. I knew that if my doctrine was wrong, I would gladly adjust it. But I was able to know that without feeling fear or lack. Very early in my walk with God I had the opportunity to decide the source of my salvation—my doctrine or my Savior.

Doctrine can be an illusion. In our cerebral, egocentric world, we choose doctrines like we pick out new clothes. We decide which one looks best on us, and that's the one we

*In our cerebral, egocentric world,
we choose doctrines like we pick out new clothes.*

select. We have no sense of putting what we believe to the test. Rather, we look to the approval of some group to validate our doctrine.

The Doctrinal Test

Jesus said when we put the truth into practice, we would experience that truth and then it would set us free.[2] How do we know if our doctrine is truth? I have learned that my doctrine must be validated through at least three sources. First I must be sure it is consistent with the Word of God as a whole. Then I must make sure that it does not violate what Jesus did through His death, burial, and resurrection. Third, I must consider its consistency with the life of Jesus. Only then am I ready to proceed to the realm of personal experience.

If my doctrine stands the test of these three benchmarks, then I have to ask myself, "What is this adding to my life? Is this setting me free or taking me captive? Jesus said He came to give me life to its fullest. Will believing what I believe contribute to

---

2. See John 8:31–32.

the quality of my life? How does it make me feel about me?" Demeaning doctrines that rob us of dignity and worth have no place in the kingdom of God.

Jesus also said that everything about God is summed up in two realities: Love God and love people.[3] I have to consider, does what I believe about God make me love Him more? Does it make me have more value for God? Does it endear me to Him? Likewise, I have to ask, does it make me love people more? Are my beliefs making me more tolerant, patient, and kind? If not, then something is not as it should be.

*Demeaning doctrines that rob us of dignity
and worth have no place in the kingdom of God.*

The starting place of all transformation is a change of opinion (repentance) about righteousness. Until I believe that God has an accepting view of me, I cannot have a healthy sense of self. Apart from faith righteousness, all growth is viewed as change that must be done in order to satisfy a displeased God. Apart from faith righteousness, every positive aspect of the Christian life takes on a negative connotation.

*The starting place of all transformation is a
change of opinion (repentance) about righteousness.*

Accepting Jesus as your righteousness should be the cornerstone of your new understanding of God. The very foundation of salvation itself rests in what people believe about righteousness. Unfortunately, most new believers are never

---

3.   See Matthew 22:37–40.

introduced to this all-important reality. If you have been in church for years, then moving from the place of trusting your works to a place of trusting the righteousness of God may require overcoming years of religious conditioning.

Revelation Is a New Perspective

We need revelation in order to see what we do not see. The eyes of our heart must be open in order to move from where we are to where we want to go! Sadly, the concept of seeking revelation has been perverted by the idea that we must somehow convince God to show us what He previously has not been willing to show us. Our faulty, "need-based theology" creates the illusion that revelation is something God must bring to us. We, like Adam and Eve, have come to believe there is something God has not given us or shown us that would make our lives so much better. It is, in fact, that belief has blinded us to what He already has given us in Jesus.

That crippling concept is in direct opposition to the Word of God. The Word says, *"His divine power hath given unto us all things that pertain unto life and godliness, through the knowledge of him that hath called us to glory and virtue"* (2 Peter 1:3 KJV). God has already given me everything I need in Jesus. In order to draw upon those internal resources, I must make sure that I am growing in my knowledge of Him and His finished work.

It was this mind-set of lack that led Adam and Eve into unbelief and mistrust. To believe that God is "holding out" on us is a direct affront to His character. When we believe this, we

To believe that God is "holding out"
on us is a direct affront to His character.

deny every promise of the completed work of Jesus and call out to God to show us what He seemingly has not yet shown.

We refuse to accept that our opinions and doctrines are the only things limiting our perception of God and His provision.

Revelation is not when God shows us what He, up until that time, has been withholding from us. Revelation is what we see when we change our position by surrendering our opinion. A change of position always brings a change in perception. When I step out from behind my opinion I am able to see that which was not previously clear. If my religious views are the source of my safety and confidence, however, I will not

*A change of position always
brings a change in perception.*

surrender them. Instead, I will defend them though they destroy me. So often we stand behind our opinion and then wonder why we cannot see clearly. We cry out for God to move on our behalf and show us, but God has cried out for us to repent so we can see.

God desires that we see and experience all that Jesus died to give us. The New Testament is a revelation, not a mystery. Blindness and limited understanding are always related to the heart. In 2 Corinthians 3:14–16 Paul told us how the law became a veil that limited Israel's view of God. Embracing any opinion that is not based on New Testament revelation does not show us God. Rather, it limits our view of God.

Jesus, the *logos* of God, showed us who God is. In Him everything that we have understood about God comes together. Yet, we reject what He showed us and look back to the law to see God. We make ourselves disciples of Moses instead of Jesus. We reject Him as the wisdom of God and lean to our own understanding, which is derived from the law. We reject God's revelation that He gave us in Jesus and seek our own private revelation.

Reshape Your Heart

Paul, though, showed us how the veil of opinion can be removed. *"But even unto this day, when Moses is read, the veil is upon their heart. Nevertheless when it shall turn to the Lord, the veil shall be taken away"* (2 Corinthians 3:15–16 KJV). The veil to which Paul referred was trust in the Old Covenant. The people thought the law could make them righteous, or acceptable to God. As a result, they were afraid to release what they thought would make them acceptable to God. The truth is, when people look to the law for their righteousness, they bind themselves to a blinding sense of lack. It is like an addict who hates his drug but has to have it in order to function. It has become a part of the fabric of his life. When the law is our confidence, it alters our view of God and dictates our understanding of the New Covenant.

The Bible says, *"A froward heart cannot find good"* (Proverbs 17:20 KJV). The word *froward* literally means "crooked." It seems that pain, sorrow, and religion have the ability to distort the shape of the heart. When the heart has been "bent" by religion, pain, and sorrow, it distorts our perception. Like light passing through a prism, that which is clear and bright changes colors when it is bent. Truth that enters our heart is bent to facilitate the beliefs of our heart. It shades everything we see. It alters ours perception. In 2 Corinthians 3:16 when Paul said, *"When **it** shall turn to the Lord…"* (KJV), he was talking about the heart. The verse literally means when the heart is "twisted back," the veil is taken away.

The only thing that has the power to "twist" your heart back into the shape that God intended it to be is the righteousness of Jesus. A heart that is established in faith righteousness does not twist the truth to accommodate its fear and insecurity. It has no sense of lack or rejection.

God has already filled you with the knowledge of His will. All His wisdom is in you now. The challenge is yielding to Him in a way that allows your heart to "twist back" to its true shape so that it can facilitate the revelation of the truth. Our heart must be made straight by accepting the righteousness of Jesus as our own. Make faith righteousness the breastplate that guards your heart against every fiery dart.[4]

A heart that is established in faith righteousness does not twist the truth to accommodate its fear and insecurity.

As you daily implement the suggested steps at the end of each chapter, you will find your heart turning back to Jesus. As He becomes yours source of righteousness, your concepts of God will change. You will step from behind your self-righteousness to a wide-open world of faith righteousness. You will see and understand what you have never seen before. You will be freed from your opinion, liberated by a revelation of Jesus, led by a new understanding of His Word, and empowered by faith righteousness.

---

4.   See Ephesians 6:14.

CHAPTER 13

IS JESUS ENOUGH?

For years we have touted the slogan, "Jesus is the answer." We have assured the world, "Jesus is all you need." Yet, immediately after our conversion, we were led to believe that Jesus was not actually enough…. He was not enough to make us secure with God. He was not enough to qualify us for the promises of God. He was not enough to make us accepted by God.

I know you would argue, "No one ever told me Jesus was not enough." Although it is certainly true that no one in the church would ever utter those words, the moment you were told that you had to do things to qualify for these promises, you accepted the idea that Jesus was indeed not enough. You were persuaded to believe that Jesus plus your works was enough.

Satan never actually told Adam and Eve that God was a liar. He simply led them to ask questions that caused them to reach false conclusions. The assumption they reached was that God had not given them everything they needed for a quality life. This conclusion connected them to a false sense of lack that began to drive their logic and subsequent actions.

Jesus Plus…

The apostle Paul was astonished that the believers at Galatia had been seduced into thinking Jesus was not enough. He said, *"I am astonished that you are so quickly deserting the one who called you by the grace of Christ and are turning to a different gospel—which is really no gospel at all"* (Galatians 1:6–7 NIV). No one ever said they were offering them a different gospel. No one ever said there was anything wrong with the gospel they had received. All it took to bring them to a place where Jesus no longer affected their life[1] was to get them to add something to their source of confidence! Jesus plus anything disconnects you from Jesus as your source. It is sort of like telling your wife you will be faithful except for the times you commit adultery. That is not faithfulness.

> *Jesus plus anything disconnects you from Jesus as your source.*

These false preachers in the book of Galatians didn't get the believers to do something bad. They go them to do something good, something that was in the Scriptures. The problem was not what they did. The problem was that they began to trust in their works to make them righteous, thereby neutralizing God's grace (ability) in their lives.[2]

A religious group, who preached Jesus, came after Paul and insisted that while Jesus was enough to get them born again, they could expect God to keep His promises only if they upheld righteousness through the law. The same group told the church at Colosse that if they failed to keep some part of the law, it would open the door to the devil. He would have the right to attack them.

Paul wrote the letters to the Galatians and the Colossians to bring them back to the place of grace, peace, and faith

---

1. Galatians 5:4: "*Christ is become of no effect unto you, whosoever of you are justified by the law; ye are fallen from grace*" (KJV).

2. Galatians 2:21: "*I do not frustrate the grace of God: for if righteousness come by the law, then Christ is dead in vain*" (KJV).

righteousness. They had abandoned their trust in Jesus by adding the need to trust in the law. They surrendered faith righteousness for works righteousness. Although they verbalized an allegiance to Jesus, it was mere lip service. They no longer followed Him as Lord or Savior.

Righteousness is what qualifies us for salvation, for the promises of God, and for all God's provision. Trusting Jesus as our righteousness is what makes Him our Savior. Trusting Him enough to follow His teaching and become a disciple is what makes Him our Lord. Therefore, whatever we trust for righteousness becomes our savior. When we trust obedience to the law to make us righteous, we have made ourselves our savior. Our sacrifice of obedience is what purchases our salvation instead of Jesus' sacrifice of obedience.

When we trust our logic of performance more than the logic of God, which was expressed through Jesus, we become our own lord. Thus we have the ultimate fulfillment of Adam's sin: We become the god of our own world, knowing good and evil for ourselves. In this case we have said that our

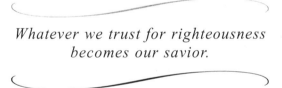

*Whatever we trust for righteousness
becomes our savior.*

way is good and God's way is evil. I realize that we never say those words, but our life expresses them. Our source of trust proves them to be true.

The Most Important Question

This is the single most important question we must ask ourselves: Is Jesus enough? On an intellectual level Jesus is certainly enough. We all can quote scriptures and parrot all the "spiritually correct" clichés. However, let's ask this question another way: Is Jesus enough to make me feel right with God?

Does my relationship with Him satisfy all my sense of lack and inadequacy? Do I have complete peace with God? Does His sacrifice qualify me for all the promises of God? Where is

> *This is the single most important question we must ask ourselves: Is Jesus enough?*

my trust—in His performance or mine? In Romans 5:1 Paul said, *"Having been justified by faith, we have peace with God through our Lord Jesus Christ."* When our justification before God has its roots in the righteousness of Jesus, we can abide in His presence in total peace. A sense of completeness will permeate our life.

This is exactly what Paul meant in Romans 1:17 when he said, *"The righteousness of God is revealed from faith to faith."* And we could safely add, not from faith to works. Paul asked the Galatians, *"Are you so foolish? After beginning with the Spirit, are you now trying to attain your goal by human effort?"* (Galatians 3:3 NIV) We start our walk trusting God's Spirit to work in us, then are deceived into thinking we must complete the work by our personal efforts. How could anyone experience God's incredible saving power as a free gift and then abandon Jesus? Simple—someone gets you asking the wrong questions so that you connect yourself to the sense of lack.

No one ever says, "Jesus is not enough," or, "Don't trust Jesus for your righteousness." They simply appeal to your natural (carnal) logic, which Paul said cannot grasp the logic of God. In fact, he said this:

> *Those who live according to the flesh set their minds on the things of the flesh, but those who live according to the Spirit, the things of the Spirit. For to be carnally minded is death, but to be spiritually minded is life and peace. Because*

*the carnal mind is enmity against God; for it is not subject
to the law of God, nor indeed can be. So then, those who
are in the flesh cannot please God* (Romans 8:5–8).

Being "in the flesh" is a scriptural term. It describes people who trust in the "works of the flesh"; that is, in their natural abilities to make them righteous. In an attempt to break through their logic Paul asked, *"I would like to learn just one thing from you: Did you receive the Spirit by observing the law, or by believing what you heard?"* (Galatians 3:2 NIV) It's a simple question. "When you got born again, did it happen because you earned it or because you believed what you heard?"

Paul was attempting to connect them once again to the sense of wholeness they originally had found in Jesus by asking them the appropriate questions. They were made righteous enough that God's Spirit came and dwelt in them as a free gift. It is like asking, "If God gave us the best He had for free, why would He make us pay for anything else?" In Romans Paul said it like this: *"He that spared not his own Son, but delivered him up for us all, how shall he not with him also freely give us all things?"* (Romans 8:32 KJV) Paul's questions were designed to bring people back to Jesus. The answers are obvious.

*If God gave us the best He had for free,
why would He make us pay for anything else?*

God wants us to trust the sacrifice of Jesus. He wants us to receive a quality of righteousness that is so pure that it will qualify us for all God has and will empower us to live as we should. He wants us to have a righteousness that is ours apart from our performance, a righteousness that is found only in Jesus. This is why Jesus said, *"Unless your righteousness exceeds the righteousness of the scribes and Pharisees, you will by no means enter the kingdom of heaven"* (Matthew 5:20).

Just think of it—those who depend on their works for righteousness have no hope of entering the kingdom of heaven. Yet, they manipulate those whose faith righteousness is far superior to what they have. Paul said those who look to the flesh have always persecuted those who look to the Spirit.[3] They need you to give up your confidence as a way to boost theirs.

Rejoice in your righteousness. Every time you have a prayer answered, every time something goes right, remind yourself that you are qualified by the finished work of Jesus. The more you magnify Jesus as your righteousness, the more you connect to wholeness and leave lack and all its destructive power behind. The more you remind yourself that Jesus is enough, the more He becomes your everything!

---

3. See Galatians 4:22–30.

CHAPTER 14

OVERCOMING SHAME AND CONFUSION

As Danny told me his story of personal failure, my heart broke. This man, who had once served God so boldly, now could not look me in the eye. Before me sat only the shell of the previous confident believer he had once been. Guilt for his actions had long since been overcome by shame. No matter where he went or what he did, he had the abiding awareness of his past sins.

The body of Christ didn't really help him much. It seemed that no matter where he went, there was still someone who was more than willing to reject him because of his past sin. Everyone expressed so much concern that he pay the price for his sin that no one considered helping him out of his pain. In fact, it appeared that people believed he had truly repented only if he remained in pain and shame.

Too many times we think shame is a form of humility, a proof of repentance. In reality a person can experience deep remorse without yielding to a life of shame. Only when we see people with their heads hung low are we willing to believe they have repented of their wrong. Nothing could be farther from the truth. If people had actually repented, they would hold their head high and reclaim their identity in Jesus.

We want people who have failed to live in shame as proof that they are aware of their sin. And that is exactly what shame is. Shame is a negative emotion that controls our life by keeping us in constant awareness of our sin. Living in awareness of sin is what the law does for us. This is not, however, the work of the Holy Spirit in the New Testament. He is here to make us aware of the fact that we are now righteous in Jesus. No matter what our past is, or how recent it is, we can rise above it and live the quality of life that Jesus promised.

Shame keeps us in the cycle. It keeps us connected to the sins of the past. It ensures that we will commit those sins again. It insists that we define our life by our personal failures. It is an emotional connection with everything from which Jesus died to free us. It not only says, "This is what you have done," but it also says, "This is who you are; this is who you will always be."

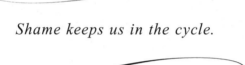

Shame keeps us in the cycle.

Few things are more destructive than shame. Shame robs you of the sense of dignity and worth. It paralyzes you in the past. It disempowers you from living a new and different future. It intoxicates you with confusion. It clouds your mind with an emotional stupor that leads to horrible decision-making. It keeps you in a never-ending cycle of negative emotions, negative decisions, and negative results.

Feelings Drive Actions

Thoughts and beliefs generate emotions. Emotions drive our thought processes and ultimately our actions. Every action we take is based on a combination of logic and emotion. We occasionally make decisions that contradict our emotions. But, in the end, we always fall back to the feelings that are driving us. Emotions continually stir us to some type of action.

I have heard it said that feelings are a call to action.[1] I believe that is absolutely true. Feelings always lead us to an action

---

1.   Anthony Robbins, *Get the Edge*, audiotape series (San Diego, CA: Robbins Research International, 2000).

of some kind. When a person says, "I am led by faith, not by feelings," that is only a partial truth. One is wrapped up in the power of the other. How? Faith is simply trust. It is based on your beliefs. Those beliefs cause feelings, and those feelings lead your actions. You can never totally escape the role that feelings play in our decisions. What we need is faith in God's promises. That faith then produces strong positive feelings that play a role in empowering us to take actions consistent with those promises.

> *Every action we take is based*
> *on a combination of logic and emotion.*

People who live in guilt and shame seldom make quality decisions unless they understand the difference between the two. Guilt is the feeling we have when we violate our conscience. It is a negative emotion. A negative emotion is not a call to negative action. Sadly, though, when people feel negative emotions, they tend to be moved to negative actions. Sometimes those actions are thinking more negative thoughts. Often they are bona fide negative actions. In reality, negative emotions are a call to a different kind of action.

Guilt tells me I have taken an inappropriate action and that I must change my action. Guilt is like a warning light in your car. It is telling you that whatever you are doing, you must stop now or the engine will break down. Negative emotions simply tell me I must initiate a positive, life-giving action. Otherwise I will plunge myself into a cycle of destructive thoughts, feelings, and actions.

Shame is something altogether different. When you study the Hebrew language, you find several Hebrew words for shame. One seems to point more toward disgrace. Another indicates a feeling of vileness or ignominy, humiliation, confusion, and embarrassment. Interestingly, the same Hebrew word for shame is also used of an idol. Shame becomes an idol. It is something that denies the truth of God's Word. It defies the reality of faith righteousness. It cries out, "I am more powerful than the blood of Jesus. I am more real than the resurrection!" When we yield to shame, it is synonymous with

A negative emotion is not a call to negative action.

bowing down to an idol. We have exalted our vain imagination and our tormented emotions above the knowledge of God. We commit to those negative feelings as a higher reality than God's Word.

Shame is like a self-induced punishment for our wrongs. Many people feel they should live in shame in order to pay for their wrongs. Ironically, one can never suffer enough to pay the cost. When is enough ever enough? The price for our negative actions keeps rising. The more we think about our sin, the more we think we should pay. The more we feel shame, the less deserving we feel of God's love and mercy. There is no end to shame.

In order to continue to feel shame we must have a continual awareness of our failure. People who live in shame rehearse their failures over and over again. They keep those failures alive in their mind and emotions. This is exactly what Paul identified as a weakness of the law. The law gives us the knowledge of sin.[2] The awareness of sin keeps the negative emotions associated with sin ever present. Those emotions keep us connected to the sense of lack. The sense of lack is what keeps us bound to the power of sin. It keeps us in our destructive, repetitive cycles.

---

2.   See Romans 3:20.

There is a biblical principle that says, "What you think on grows in your life." I like to say it this way: "You become what you behold." People who live in shame are forever attached to their past sins and failures. Because they keep those things alive in their heart, they are still subject to them. Shame binds us to the sins of the past. It ensures that we will eventually repeat the same sin.

Guilt is an initial emotional response to inappropriate behavior. It is a call to take another action. Shame is an immersion in guilt; it tells us that we are what we have done. Shame says this is who we are; guilt says what we have done is inappropriate. The ability to separate our actions from our identity is a paradox wrapped in a mystery. But, that ability is essential to emotional health and stability.

The Solution to Shame

When we sin, it is essential that we own that sin, that we acknowledge it. First John 1:9 tells us to confess our sin. The word *confess* simply means to "say the same thing." I must say the same thing about my sin that God says. He says that sin has no power over me.[3] He says that I have a new nature. He says that I am righteous; therefore, I have no excuse for sin. After I confess my sin, I must then walk in the light. Walking in the light, or the truth, begins not by focusing on what I have done wrong but acknowledging the same thing God says about it.

First John 1:7 says, *"But if we walk in the light as He is in the light, we have fellowship with one another, and the blood of Jesus Christ His Son cleanses us from all sin."* Walking in the light always brings a person back to the place of fellowship with Jesus. Acknowledging that I am righteous, accepting God's forgiveness, is of little value if that does not facilitate my return

---

3.   Romans 6:14: *"For sin shall not be your master, because you are not under law, but under grace"* (NIV).

to intimacy with Jesus. It is intimacy with Jesus that restores my soul and gives me my life back!

Even when I have sinned, I must still acknowledge that I am righteous in Jesus. I must acknowledge that sin has no power over me, and that as a righteous being I have no excuse

Walking in the light, or the truth, begins not by focusing on what I have done wrong but acknowledging the same thing God says about it.

for sin. I also must acknowledge God's desire to fellowship with me. I have to reverse all the emotions that are trying to convince me that I am now separated from God.

Sin does not actually separate a person from God, but it makes one "feel" separated. Colossians 1:21 says that our wicked works alienate us from God *in our mind*. Under the Old Covenant sin did separate us from God. Under the New

Even when I have sinned, I must still acknowledge that I am righteous in Jesus.

Covenant nothing can separate us from the love of God.[4] However, if I allow those feelings of separation and guilt to call me to more negative action, I will end up in the grip of shame. I will deny my new identity in Jesus. I may never really recover. I will be like Adam who hid from God when He walked through the Garden calling out for fellowship. Yes, even after

---

4.   Romans 8:38–39: *"For I am persuaded that neither death nor life, nor angels nor principalities nor powers, nor things present nor things to come, nor height nor depth, nor any other created thing, shall be able to separate us from the love of God which is in Christ Jesus our Lord."*

we have sinned, God wants to restore the relationship. He always pursues us and calls us back. Like the father of the prodigal, His love for us never changes.

Sin, though, robs us of confidence. The apostle John told the church that walking in love would put our heart at rest when we are in God's presence.[5] So sin does not have the ability to make God stop loving us. It does not have the power to separate us from God. It does, however, have the power to affect our thoughts and feelings so that we feel separated from God!

*Sin does not actually separate a person
from God, but it makes one "feel" separated.*

Faith always looks back to the finished work of Jesus. That is reality, no matter what I feel. As I acknowledge who I am in Jesus, I change my emotions and ultimately I change my actions. Exercising my faith, by acknowledging my righteousness in Christ, lifts me from the confusion of shame. I am once again able to see reality from God's perspective.

Isaiah spoke of this day of righteousness when he prophesied about the Spirit of the Lord upon Jesus. He said, *"The Spirit of the Lord God is upon Me...to console those who mourn in Zion, to give them beauty for ashes, the oil of joy for mourning, the garment of praise for the spirit of heaviness; that they may be called trees of righteousness, the planting of the Lord, that He may be glorified"* (Isaiah 61:1,3). Our righteousness is of God. We look to Him. We glorify Him. We honor Him because we know that this is His work. We are planted by the Lord.

I must always be aware of the fact that I am the righteousness of God. I have the power to make good decisions and the

---

5.   See 1 John 3:19.

power to see them through. Shame is not a tool that God uses to teach me; rather it is something for which Jesus died to set me free. As I remind myself that I am righteous in Jesus, confusion, shame, and guilt disappear. I once again return to God's reality and experience freedom from the shame of the past.

In faith righteousness we find that paradox of accepting responsibility for our actions yet being freed from the debilitating power of those actions. We feel guilt and disappointment without disempowerment. The negative feelings serve as a wake-up call to return to righteousness instead of a blind guide that leads us into the ditch.

Acknowledge that guilt and shame are not something you must live with as payment for your wrong. Instead, acknowledge that Jesus' death was the payment for your wrong. Say, "I believe in the blood of Jesus more than I believe in my sacrifices. I am righteous through Jesus. I will not live in the past. I will live a new, powerful life of peace and godliness. I will yield to the righteousness that is in me through Jesus." Say this every time guilt and shame try to define your life. Paul said it this way: *"That the communication of thy faith may become effectual by the acknowledging of every good thing which is in you in Christ Jesus"* (Philemon 6 KJV). Never stop acknowledging all the good things that are in you through Jesus. It is your connection to righteousness and wholeness.

CHAPTER 15

THE BLIND LEADING THE BLIND

A t this point, one has to ask, "Why aren't we moving on? Why doesn't the church simply read the pages of the New Testament, believe them, and break into a life of complete freedom and victory?"

Simple! We are trapped in the cycle of lack, failure, guilt, and shame. Because we have believed the lie of works righteousness, we are not bold enough to break away from the deception that cripples us. We are like the baby elephant whose trainers control him through a chain attached to a small stake driven in the ground. When he grows to full strength he could easily pull up the stake and break away. But he has been attached to the stake for so long that he doesn't know he is able to easily find his freedom. Like an elephant tied to a stick, we hold to religious ideas that don't work, all the while despising what they do to our lives. Ironically, the sense of lack and fear that is created by this corrupt doctrine makes us afraid to trust Jesus as our righteousness. In short, we are afraid of the cure! We want to run to home plate but we're afraid to take our foot off of third!

I once heard an illustration that demonstrates this destructive cycle. A group of people all made a genuine commitment to be disciples and students of a particular discipline. But in their desire to preserve tradition and avoid loss of approval, they ended up simply following one another. They were like men walking in a circle, each one following the one in front of him, but they all were actually following one another. Although this has the appearance of a committed life, it is a deception. They all were moving, but going nowhere! Following someone doesn't mean you are going anywhere.

Paul said that we should follow those who by *"faith and patience inherit the promises"* (Hebrews 6:12 KJV). We have not qualified our leaders according to the Bible. Many of us didn't even study the Bible for ourselves, but simply followed our leaders into darkness. Now we are afraid to let go of their hands. We are like the offspring of child molesters. They may be the ones hurting us, but they are the only parents we know. They provide enough security to make us justify our pain. Take a moment now and think about it. Who are you following? Whose doctrine has molded your concept of God? What do they really believe about God? How do you see Jesus as your righteousness once they have influenced your thoughts?

*Following someone doesn't
mean you are going anywhere.*

Recently a close friend and ministry associate arrived at my home. As we shared the events of the day, he told me a story that took place on his drive to my home. He said, "As I drove, I listened to a tape set of one of my favorite teachers. It started out very good. But as the message progressed, it veered from reality. The person began to tell how God had put them through certain difficulties so they would have compassion on those who faced similar hardships."

My friend couldn't believe his ears. Before being established in faith righteousness, that kind of teaching would have gone unquestioned. It would have subtly crept into his beliefs. It would have gone unchallenged and undetected but not without consequences. The next time he faced a hardship, he would have begun to question, "Is this something I should accept or resist? Did Jesus set me free from this or is Jesus doing this to me?" Confidence would have been lost. Boldness would have faded away in the dark questioning of religious confusion.

That which goes unquestioned eventually is accepted as reality! Through a lack of awareness of the completed work of Jesus, we accept that which undermines and contradicts Jesus' finished work. We are like the people in the example I used earlier. We are earnestly following the person in front of us. He is earnestly following the one in front of him, and so on. But none of us are going anywhere other than where we have already been. As Jesus said, we are *"like sheep without a shepherd"* (Matthew 9:36 NIV).

This endless, pointless walking in circles is the picture that comes to my mind when I think of the religious world. Jesus said it this way: *"If the blind leads the blind, both will fall into a ditch"* (Matthew 15:14). The church world cannot break free from its present limitations because to do so would risk the loss of religious approval. We would have to break out of the circle. We would lose the false sense of comfort that comes from following the crowd.

*The church world cannot break free
from its present limitations because to do so
would risk the loss of religious approval.*

A Sense of Completeness

While fear, codependency, and lack earmark those who are trapped in the cycle of works, righteousness, boldness, peace, and interdependence are fruits of faith righteousness. The fearful codependent clings to the group for the approval he or she is not experiencing in God. Such people vainly look to man to give them what only God Himself can provide: a sense of completeness.

On the other hand, those who trust the righteousness of Jesus are filled with boldness and confidence. Their sense of wholeness does not fluctuate with the approval of man. Proverbs 28:1 says it best: *"The wicked flee when no one pursues, But the righteous are bold as a lion."* The sense of righteousness (by faith) is an emotional foundation that cannot be shaken. It provides a stability that defies all logic!

The prophet Isaiah foretold of a day when mankind could live free from oppression when he said, *"In righteousness you shall be established; you shall be far from oppression, for you shall not fear"* (Isaiah 54:14). The righteousness of which he spoke is more than mere performance. Please don't misunderstand; I have great value for good works. But the righteousness of God is built on something far more eternal than my goods works.

Fear is what leads to oppression. Fear is about judgment. The Living Bible does an excellent job of translating 1 John 4:18. It says, *"We need have no fear of someone who loves us perfectly; his perfect love for us eliminates all dread of what he might do to us. If we are afraid, it is for fear of what he might do to us, and shows that we are not fully convinced that he really loves us."* Fear strips us of confidence. The assurance of unconditional love, on the other hand, is associated with boldness.

In the Old Testament, righteous living was the only level of confidence a person could obtain. If the individual did not "live right," he had no basis for boldness. In the New Testament, we receive the gift of righteousness. And if I know I am righteous, I know God can love me. If my righteousness is a gift from Him, then I abide in total peace, total confidence, and total freedom from fear. Boldness does not waver when righteousness is given as a gift.

Isaiah 54 continues to describe the life of this person who abides in righteousness. *"No weapon formed against you shall prosper, and every tongue which rises against you in judgment you shall condemn. This is the heritage of the servants of the Lord."* This place of righteousness of which Isaiah prophesied is a place where we are free from every form of fear, oppression, and condemnation. We become immune to the judgments of others.

Up to this point one could argue that Isaiah was prophesying of the righteousness that comes by our performance. But the last phrase in this prophecy clarifies any possible confusion when it says, " *'And their righteousness is from Me,' says the Lord"* (Isaiah 54:17). He is clearly speaking of this day wherein our righteousness comes from the Lord Jesus!

We have spent our lives following people who have led us into works righteousness. This doe not mean they are bad people. It does not mean they do not love God. It just means they are following the person in front of them, without qualifying their life or their message by the life and message of Jesus!

Paul or Apollos?

Not long ago I was reading about Apollos' preaching to the church at Corinth. Apollos was an eloquent speaker. He must have been a man of incredible passion because people followed him. The problem was, in spite of all his passion, he still preached an incomplete message. It was not until some of the disciples of Jesus took him aside and helped him with his doctrine that he even preached a message based on the resurrection of Jesus.[1]

Paul, on the other hand, came to Corinth with a message about the risen Savior. He preached faith righteousness. He introduced the world to the mysteries of God—Christ in you, the hope of glory. He even admitted that he was not a very eloquent speaker. In 1 Corinthians 2:1 he said, *"When I came to you, brothers, I did not come with eloquence or superior wisdom as*

---

1. See Acts 18:24–26.

I proclaimed to you the testimony about God" (NIV). In verse 3 he went on to say, *"I came to you in weakness and fear, and with much trembling"* (NIV).

This would mean very little except for the fact that years after Paul and Apollos had both preached at Corinth, there were those who rejected Paul's message and wanted to follow Apollos. Remember, when Apollos first arrived he proclaimed a very incomplete message. Paul, on the other hand, had experienced a personal encounter with Jesus. He had received a personal commission to take the Gospel to the Gentile world. He had spent more than fourteen years in personal preparation for ministry. Yet, Apollos' message was the one that many chose simply because he was the better preacher.

Who are you following, and why? Are they, like Apollos, people of great influence preaching a passionate message, yet withholding the most essential part of the message—the fact that Jesus has been raised from the dead, conquering sin, death, and hell, and is offering us the righteousness of God as a free gift? Are they making you feel empowered and safe with God? Or do they cause you to question God's unfailing love? Does their message make you feel qualified for all the promises through Jesus? Or are they making you feel that you must create your own personal qualifications through your performance? Are they making you feel safe from the fear of the devil? Or do they make you feel that you can give away the authority that Jesus obtained from His resurrection?

Who are you following, and why?

Ask yourself, as the writer of Hebrews challenged, "Do the people I follow walk in faith righteousness and receive the promises of God? Or do they try to drag me back under a works mentality to qualify for God's promise? Am I walking in a circle, blindly following the one in front of me, just because he is in the circle? Or have I chosen to follow Jesus, the author and finisher of my faith, the captain of my salvation, my righteousness, my peace, my joy? Have I really found in Him the endless source of life at its best? Have I limited my concept and my experience with God to the limits of the person I am following?" Maybe it's time to get out of the circle!

Choosing to break out of the circle does not mean you reject the people you have been following. It simply means you put them in proper perspective in your life. Do you want what they can give you or what Jesus can give you? Become a true disciple today by making the choice to follow the teaching and principles of the Lord Jesus in every area of your life.

CHAPTER 16

THE VOICE OF THE CONSCIENCE

The most common objection people present when they hear the message of faith righteousness is, "But couldn't this be abused?" Actually, I should rephrase that. Not everyone asks this question. In fact, I have never introduced a non-Christian to this good news and had him or her ask that question. Instead, the person simply falls in love with God, rejoicing in His goodness. In the heart of a person hungry for change, this message does exactly what it is intended to do: It draws people to God and empowers them to become who they desire to be.[1]

Only those hardened by religion consider the issue of abuse to be a major obstacle. Saying that faith righteousness will cause a person to be unfaithful to God is like saying, "If a man marries a merciful, loving woman, it will cause him to cheat." It could happen, but it is less likely than if she was mean and judgmental.

After one has labored under the influence of works righteousness the heart becomes hardened to the goodness of God and logic becomes twisted. When people reach the stage where they ask this question, they are already in the cycle to some degree. Their logic is driven by the sense of lack. Their thinking has already been flawed and their conscience tainted by an incomplete gospel, which Paul said was no gospel at all.[2]

---

1. Romans 2:4: *"Do you despise the riches of His goodness, forbearance, and long-suffering, not knowing that the goodness of God leads you to repentance?"*

2. See Galatians 1:6–7.

People who are truly in search of a new life realize that change is essential. Few people actually believe they can stay the same and have a better life. In fact, personal change is an

> *People who are truly in search of a new life realize that change is essential.*

incredible motivator among those who come to Jesus. They have reached the end of themselves, and they want the power to become someone new. The message of faith righteousness is the light of hope in a dark life.

Make no mistake, I too want to change. I want to be a better person. I want to treat people right. I want to live a life pleasing to God and worthy of the Gospel. I want to live above the power of sin. I greatly value these attributes, and faith righteousness at work in my heart is the only thing that has ever empowered me to live those values.

Paul put it this way: *"For we are God's workmanship, created in Christ Jesus to do good works, which God prepared in advance for us to do"* (Ephesians 2:10 NIV). There has never been a question that God wants us fully committed to a life of good works. The apostle Paul was actually accused of teaching people to sin to make God look good.[3] Those whose minds have been twisted by sin, religion, or legalism always twist the teaching of righteousness to their own destruction.

The way we live is a continuum of our beliefs. A person fully committed to following the Lord Jesus will commit to a life of good works. The problem comes, however, when we do good works because we think that's what makes us good. In so doing we try to make our good works our source of righteousness,

---

3.　Romans 3:8: *"And why not say, 'Let us do evil that good may come'?—as we are slanderously reported and as some affirm that we say."*

rather than allow our righteousness to be the source of our good works!

The carnal-minded believer looks to good works to define his righteousness. We should look at our righteousness in Jesus and allow that to define and empower us for good works. The writer of Hebrews pointed out that the very first foundational doctrine of the New Testament is repentance

We should look at our righteousness in Jesus and allow that to define and empower us for good works.

from dead works and faith toward God.[4] Before we can move on to faith in God, we first have to give up faith in our works.

When Paul spoke of repentance from dead works, he was not referring to the dead works of sin. He was referring to religious works, to the good things we do in the hopes of earning acceptance and favor with God. In Romans 10:3 he

Before we can move on to faith in God, we first have to give up faith in our works.

described the person who trusts his works for his righteousness: *"For they being ignorant of God's righteousness, and seeking to establish their own righteousness, have not submitted to the righteousness of God."*

---

4.   Hebrews 6:1: *"Therefore, leaving the discussion of the elementary principles of Christ, let us go on to perfection, not laying again the foundation of repentance from dead works and of faith toward God."*

"So where is the value for good works?" you might ask. There is so much value in committing to a life of good works. When we walk in love, we enjoy peaceful, productive relationships. When we have good manners, we tend to have less conflict. When we treat people well, they tend to return the kindness. When we pay our bills, we create financial opportunities. When we work hard, we get raises and promotions. When we apply God's rules for relationships, we experience favor. Good works primarily affect us on the horizontal plane in the way we relate to the world around us. They bring great benefit in this life! But they are the fruit, never the root.

Good Works Testify to Your Conscience

One of the great benefits of living a good, moral life is the power of a clear conscience. The conscience is like a reservoir that determines how much of God's life and power we will hold in our consciousness, and thereby experience in our life. Our conscience doesn't change the amount of God's power, it merely dictates the amount of our awareness. In so doing, it limits what we will allow ourselves to experience. Remember, whatever is present in our awareness is what we connect to emotionally.

One of the great benefits of living a good,
moral life is the power of a clear conscience.

Most of the limits that we place on God in our life revolve around our sense of self, around our perceived capacity for God. Like the children of Israel, we limit God by our limited concept of who we believe He can be in us.[5] We reduce God to our perception of what He can do through us. We create an

---

5.   Psalm 78:41: *"Yes, again and again they...limited the Holy One of Israel."*

image of God that can fit into the life we live—most of which is based on our conscience.

The word *conscience* literally means dual knowledge. Our conscience is our collective sense of self. It is this abiding sense of self that drives our life's decisions. It is how we see and experience ourselves. It is the sum total of our identity.

We create an image of God that can fit into the life we live—most of which is based on our conscience.

There are two sources of self-knowledge. There is the outer world, which is the information that comes to us from our five senses. Then there is the inner world, which is comprised of the information that comes to us through God's Spirit abiding in us. The outer world produces a knowledge of self that is based totally on circumstantial data, on our actions and our experiences in this world. The inner world produces a knowledge that comes from our sense of who we are in relation to God. These two sources of knowledge come together to form our conscience.

In order to live as God has empowered us to live, we must have a pure conscience. The voice of our outer world and the voice of our inner world must say the same thing. This happens in two ways. Paul explained one when he said that we should renew our mind after our spirit.[6] God has made our spirit perfect, completely holy and righteous. So in our mind we must see ourselves as God sees us in our spirit. Otherwise we will struggle with confidence before God. We will limit the power of righteousness. To the degree we come to see ourselves as this new righteous creation is the degree we will allow the power of righteousness to propel our lives forward.

---

6. Ephesians 4:23: *"Be renewed in the spirit of your mind"* (KJV).

Then our sense of self will be based on a spirit that has been perfected by a loving and righteous God. Additionally, our actions must say the same thing God's Spirit says about us. When our actions are inconsistent with our new identity, there is a war in our soul. Paul said it like this: *"But I see another law in my members, warring against the law of my mind, and bringing me into captivity to the law of sin which is in my members"* (Romans 7:23). The apostle Peter had this to say about the war for our soul: *"Beloved, I beg you as sojourners and pilgrims, abstain from fleshly lusts which war against the soul"* (1 Peter 2:11).

> *When our actions are inconsistent with our new identity, there is a war in our soul.*

The believer who does not manage his life well will never have a conscience that allows the righteousness of God to freely empower his life. The voice of God and the voice of his mind will be in conflict. His emotions will become distorted and confused. There will be constant inner turmoil! The apostle John gave this advice to those who struggled with their conscience: *"Dear children, let us not love with words or tongue but with actions and in truth. This then is how we know that we belong to the truth, and how we set our hearts at rest in his presence whenever our hearts condemn us"* (1 John 3:18–20 NIV). Like all the apostles, he acknowledged that a life of sin creates havoc in the soul.

John was explaining the effects of a conscience that has been disrupted by an ungodly lifestyle. Like the apostle Paul who explained how wicked works could make us feel alienated from God, John goes a bit farther to explain how our actions affect our sense of self. Just as our wicked works deny to our conscience that we have been born of God, so our good works, motivated by love, persuade our conscience that we are in fact who God says we are. Those good works become the evidence that satisfies the heart when we abide in God's presence. Those who are troubled by a guilty conscience avoid the presence of God. It is not a place that feels safe. Their heart believes these feelings are God's disapproval. But John points out that it is the condemnation of a guilty heart!

The Difference Between Being and Doing

Now, our good works do not change the reality of God. They do not add to our righteousness. But they do give us a sense of confidence when our heart condemns us. You see, the conscience is the voice of the heart. The heart is the place where the thoughts of the mind and the voice of the spirit come together to give us the dual knowledge we call our conscience. When the heart is troubled and condemned by contradictory information, we lose confidence. When our heart does not condemn us, then faith is alive and boldness abounds.

Our good works do not change the reality of God.

Because the heart is the seat of love, faith, fear, joy, and every other emotion, when it is disrupted by guilt, it can affect every aspect of our life. Thus we have the admonition from the writer of Proverbs, *"Keep your heart with all diligence, for out of it spring the issues of life"* (Proverbs 4:23). Paul told us that the wages of sin is death.[7] The first place we experience the death of sin is in our soul as our conscience condemns us, erodes our faith, and twists our heart.

John explained that there are times your heart will condemn you. Condemnation is that abiding sense of lack taken

---

7.   See Romans 6:23.

to an extreme. Condemnation is actually what you feel when you expect to be judged or rejected by God. Too often people mistakenly assume this feeling is the Holy Spirit convicting them of their sin. Nothing could be farther from the truth. Condemnation doesn't make you trust God; it makes you afraid of God. It doesn't make you run to Him; it makes you run away from Him.

I like to separate self-worth from self-confidence. Self-worth is determined by our value to God. When we see the incredible price that Jesus paid for our salvation, we begin to develop a Bible-based sense of self-worth.

> *Condemnation doesn't make you*
> *trust God; it makes you afraid of God.*

Our self-confidence, on the other hand, is based on our track record, our behavior. When we have a history of yielding to sin, then our confidence level is not so high when we face that same temptation. When we have lived inconsistently with our new righteous nature and we come into God's presence in worship or prayer, our heart will condemn us. Our guilty conscience will be conflicted, and our faith will waver.

When our spirit and soul have one voice, our heart is single and full of light. We are not divided or double-minded, our heart is at peace, and our faith is strong. This happens when the witness of the Spirit in our heart is consistent with the testimony of our life.

Our good works cannot be the ultimate basis for our confidence before God. But His Word does say it will be a factor. As such, it is a factor that we should utilize to our advantage. I am fully convinced that people who need long periods of time to "feel" the presence of God in worship and prayer are actually people who are struggling with guilt, condemnation, or just the generalized sense of lack.

Worship often becomes the price they pay to come back to God. Instead of it being a positive life-giving experience, the sense of lack turns it into dead works. Until they have paid

I am fully convinced that people who need long periods of time to "feel" the presence of God in worship and prayer are actually people who are struggling with guilt, condemnation, or just the generalized sense of lack.

what they deem to be the full price for their failure, their heart continues to condemn them. Thus the breakthrough they experience is not the presence of God flooding in; it is the release of a guilty conscience. God's presence had never left them. But their capacity to experience that presence was compromised by a guilty conscience. Remember, no matter what our conscience says, John said that *"God is greater than our heart"* (1 John 3:20). He doesn't change simply because our feelings change!

Our conscience is a natural protection against the abuse of faith righteousness. The voice of our conscience warns us when there is a contradiction between our righteous nature and our actions. But we should realize that the conscience can be seared. "To sear" means to burn, cauterize, or seal. A seared conscience is one that can no longer feel the pain of guilt. It has lost feeling through repeated use. Like a blister on the hand, over time it turns in to a callus. When we continue in sin, our hearts become callused. Eventually our conscience can no longer accurately indicate what is good and evil.

Faith in the righteousness of God connects us to God's reality. To acknowledge your righteousness in Jesus and still continue in sin leads to denial, self-deceit, and inner turmoil. It is the pathway to emotional instability. To call yourself a sinner when you have a righteous nature leads to a denial of truth and a forsaking of the power of God, thereby alienating yourself from the only power that can deliver you from sin. To call yourself righteous and live in sin brings pain and destruction. In short, there is no way to win in sin.

This dilemma is solved in one simple way. Commit yourself to a life that is based on God's Word, God's principles, and God's love. Daily renew your mind and persuade your heart

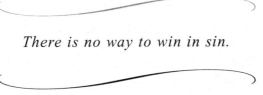

There is no way to win in sin.

that you are righteous in Jesus. Have a prayer life, a Word life, a meditation life, and a life of good works that testifies to your heart that you are righteous in Jesus.

CHAPTER 17

HEART PHYSICS

It seemed life had dealt Charlie a bad hand. He came from a disadvantaged background. He had always struggled with low self-worth. And he faced major life-obstacles. Then he made a commitment to the Lord and began attending a church that placed a continued demand on high performance. No matter how hard he tried, Charlie felt he just never measured up.

Instead of helping him to feel better about himself, his conversion and subsequent church attendance just gave him a new list of areas in which he failed to measure up. His story was not unlike many that I had heard before. He had come to our church because he found hope in a message he had heard. According to him we were his last chance before he gave up on God and on life.

I went to check on him one day because he had grown distant and stopped coming around. I was afraid his discouragement had overtaken what hope he had left. My suspicions were correct. He reluctantly allowed me into his home. After several uncomfortable minutes of evasive conversation, he blurted out, "I won't be coming around anymore."

"But, Charlie," I reasoned, "I thought we agreed that you came here to get a fresh new look at God. You were going to change the way you saw God and life. I really don't think you've given yourself a fair chance."

"It doesn't matter," he sighed. "I have too much I need to change. I sit in your services and hear all this stuff that I could have in Jesus, and it just makes me feel worse about myself. I just have too many big changes that I need to make. It's better to not even try than it is to face the demand of such huge changes."

Charlie's story is tragic and all too common. Far too many believers are in the same condition. Because of a faulty belief system, they are trapped in a darkened maze of religious demands that drown their soul in the depths of despair. How did it happen? In the parable of the sower and the seed, Jesus instructed us to take heed, to pay special attention to, to carefully consider what we hear. Why? The words that we hear are seeds that go into the soil of our heart. As we ponder them, we fertilize and water them until they grow up into a crop. And the law of the seed guarantees that the type of seed we plant is the type of crop we get.

If we plant the wrong seeds in our heart, they will grow up into a crop that traps us in our current mind-set. It is, in fact, our mind-set that traps us in the cycle of lack. In Mark 4:24 Jesus said, *"Pay attention to what you hear. The same degree of thought and study you give to what you hear determines the degree of life and virtue that comes back to you."*[1] As we think about what we hear, and even how we think about what we hear, all produces an impression on the heart.

Mark 4:25 goes on to explain, *"Whoever has will be given more; whoever does not have, even what he has will be taken from him"* (NIV). The condition of the soil is as pertinent as the seed that is sown, for the soil of the heart determines what will grow. It determines how you will interpret what you hear. In other words, your heart creates a paradigm that makes you understand everything in light of what you already believe. Therefore, you can only get more of what you have. Without a

---

1. My combination of the *Amplified, New International Version,* and original language.

*Your heart creates a paradigm that makes you under-
stand everything in light of what you already believe.*

change of heart, the person who lives in lack will go deeper
into lack.

The Missing Ingredient

The heart factor is the essential ingredient that has been
missing from the church's equation of faith. What we believe
on a conscious, deliberate level is not what will dictate our life.
It is what we believe at the heart level. The heart is that place
of "other than consciousness." It is the abode of the deep beliefs. The beliefs of the heart are directly linked to our sense of
self. It is the beliefs of the heart that determine our view of
God and the world. It is the seat of faith, fear, love, and every
other emotion. No matter what you decide on a conscious
level, you will always revert to the beliefs of the heart...unless
you know how to influence your heart.

We have the power to influence our heart. When we were
born again, our heart was made new. The slate was wiped
clean. We had the opportunity, for a brief period, to establish
a sense of identity, a level of faith, and a life of wholeness of
our choosing. All we would have needed to do to experience
every conceivable miracle in the Word of God would be to
renew our mind. By changing how and what we think, we
would have protected our heart.

Had we renewed our mind to see ourselves as a new creation, we would have experienced incredible realities in
Christ. Paul said it like this: *"Be renewed in the spirit of your
mind, and that you put on the new man which was created according to God, in true righteousness and holiness"* (Ephesians
4:23–24). We have to renew our mind to see who God has

made us in our spirit. Our task, after being born again, was not to *become* holy and righteous. Our task was to put on holiness and righteousness by changing the way we think, the way we see ourselves.

When we continue to see ourselves as we were, we re-plant those old seeds of rejection, corruption, and fear that ruled our life. In time our heart is once again corrupted with the old self-conception. This is why we lose the initial excitement and joy of our salvation. Our sense of self is confused. The voice of God in our spirit that testifies that all is well with God and us is now hearing the voice of the mind saying, "No, we are as we always have been. We are unholy. We are not righteous."

Charlie, like so many people, was confused about his power to bring about change. When he was first saved, change seemed to come easily. After being saved for a while, it seemed more difficult to bring about even the smallest of victories. His every struggle connected him more concretely to the sense of lack. It reaffirmed the false idea that he was not righteous. It trapped him in the cycle of lack. He had gone through every kind of counseling. He had tried every "spiritual formula." He now faced changes that he felt were too monumental to consider making in light of his repeated personal failures.

Take a Quantum Leap

I introduced Charlie to the principle of Heart Physics.™ Heart Physics™ is based on the principle that every law of the universe is a revelation of the character and wisdom of God. As we understand how things work in the natural world, we will understand parallel principles with God. Paul said it like this: *"For since the creation of the world God's invisible qualities— his eternal power and divine nature—have been clearly seen, being understood from what has been made"* (Romans 1:20 NIV).

Quantum physics tells us that the way to bring about the greatest change is to make it happen on the smallest level. Most people don't work that way. Instead, they try to make the big changes. They attempt too much at one time. For example, if you wanted to cure cancer, you should adjust the way you eat. You could implement a regular exercise program. Then you must take control your environment to protect you from all pollutants. That method sounds as complicated as some of the formulas for overcoming sin. Although there is validity to such approaches, it is too demanding for most people. The quantum approach would be far more simple and effective.

Quantum medicine would seek to eradicate cancer by going to the smallest level of existence. If one aspect of the code in the DNA chain could be changed, it is possible that an individual would never develop the capacity to facilitate cancer. By creating change at the smallest level, the problem could be prevented with little effort on the external level. (Some believe this will be the future of medicine.)

For years man devised weapons of mass destruction by attempting to make larger bombs, bigger explosions. But at the end of World War II the concept of quantum change rocked the world. The atomic bomb brought staggering consequences— and it was the result of splitting the atom. Massive change happens by affecting the smallest parts.

In Heart Physics™ we seek to bring about change at the smallest level. Our years of research and experimentation reveal that change at the most fundamental level produces

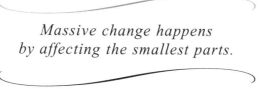

*Massive change happens
by affecting the smallest parts.*

change throughout every aspect of the human existence. We have seen people with lifelong drug addictions get immediate freedom by changing what they believe about themselves. We have seen those who have been ravaged by lifelong illness deal with one root issue and find a life of health and freedom from pain. Years of counseling focused on the heart has proven that great changes can happen because of changes at the smallest level...the level of the heart.

So, what is that incredibly small change that can happen at the very core of a person's existence that will bring dramatic, effortless transformation at every level? Simple! A change in the beliefs of the heart concerning righteousness is the quantum factor that creates limitless change. Changing what you believe about righteousness is like making an adjustment in your spiritual and emotional DNA.

The willingness to accept faith righteousness is at the core of every New Testament promise. Accepting or rejecting faith righteousness influences the capacity to receive every promise of God. It answers the single question, "What qualifies me to receive from God?" How we answer that question affects every life decision.

A change in the beliefs of the heart
concerning righteousness is the
quantum factor that creates limitless change.

The beginning point of removing every limit in life starts with a heart that is fully persuaded, completely permeated with, and totally committed to faith righteousness. Like Charlie, I have seen people who were over the edge, who had tried everything, who were ready to give up, find the solutions they needed when they changed this one thing.

Instead of attempting changes that you have never been able to make, consider taking the quantum leap. Take control over the one thing that you can do something about: your thoughts. Study the New Testament scriptures about faith righteousness. Daily meditate on and ponder these scriptures. Refuse to see yourself in any light that is not based on who you are in Jesus. When you do, you will break out of the cycle and free yourself from the sense of lack. Your view of life will change and you will be filled with confidence and peace. Just this simple quantum adjustment will introduce you to the world of permanent, painless, effortless transformation!

CHAPTER 18

A RADICAL GOSPEL

"This just sounds too good to be true!" Jackie insisted. "How could this be true and I've never heard it before? I've been in church all my life. I just don't know if I can accept this."

"I understand your feelings, " I assured her. "But I have one question for you. Is what you believe working?"

"That's kind of insensitive," she fired back even as her eyes cut through me with the look of betrayal. "You know it's not working. If it were working, I wouldn't be in your office spilling my guts. And I certainly didn't expect you to throw it in my face."

"I'm not throwing anything in your face," I replied. "It is simply time for you to ask yourself the hard questions. If what you believe doesn't work, you only have two choices. You can repent, change your mind about what you believe, or you can stay where you are."

I can't tell you how many times I've had this conversation. Thousands of desperate people have sat across from me, complaining that what they believed didn't work, but when they heard the Gospel—the great news of faith righteousness—it was too good for them to believe. When faced with the realization that they would have to change what they believe, many people have opted to continue to live in their pain.

The mind is an incredible tool that can work either for us or against us. Like every other aspect of the human entity, the mind is designed to keep us living pain-free. It seeks to resolve our issues by finding equilibrium. In other words, it has to have a way to validate our thoughts and experiences. This is why, when we believe something to be true, our mind goes into selective processing to eliminate information that would disprove our point of view.

Here's another example. When something foreign or stressful comes into our life, we are warned by the feelings of aggravation, or threat. These are crucial warning signs. However, if we continue to expose ourselves to the threat, our mind becomes desensitized. It would be too destructive and too painful for us to live under a constant, heightened sense of threat.

It is as if our mind goes through stages when dealing with threat. At first we are alerted. Then we stop noticing it. After a while we accept it as normal. Eventually we need it in order to function. Then we resist giving up what could actually be killing us. It is like the person who thinks he works better under stress. He really doesn't. Nothing about the body or mind works well under stress. However, if he has lived under stress to the point where it seems normal, he is probably addicted to it. He doesn't feel normal without it. Although it is destroying his health, diminishing his productivity, and creating chaos in his life, like every junkie, he thinks he has to have it.

A Destructive Addiction

This is what we have done with the religious beliefs that are destroying us. We have so woven them into our concept of God that we have no sense of knowing God apart from these doctrines. Earlier in my life I was a member of an organization that was very controlling. Control was a part of this group's view of God. Of course, the word *control* was never used. Rather, they talked about "spiritual authority." It is amazing how we can attach biblical terminology to an unscriptural idea, and people swallow it "hook, line, and sinker."

Everyone who didn't toe the line was labeled a rebel. These people were slandered and ostracized. No one ever left the organization on good terms. The leadership felt that they spoke the will of God for all the people and that everyone should acknowledge it and follow along. Hundreds of good people were destroyed by the destructive doctrines.

Ironically, those who were hurt the worst were usually the ones who went out and attempted to build ministries on the same principles that had brought so much pain into their own lives. They somehow thought these destructive principles would be different if they were the ones at the helm. They refused to face the fact that what they believed didn't work! They didn't know how to approach ministry without these concepts. They perpetuated the doctrines that destroyed them and multiplied them into the lives of others.

The truth is we have accepted these destructive ideas into our life. They have become a part of our self-perception and a part of our God-perception. We have had them in our life for so long that we built a system of living that allows for these destructive ideas and beliefs. We are addicted to them and do not know how to relate to God or life without them. I have found a mystery among men...everyone wants things to be different, but no one wants to change!

Without making a conscious decision about it, we become more committed to our doctrine than to Jesus. Instead of the

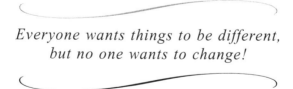

Everyone wants things to be different,
but no one wants to change!

Bible being a bridge that leads us to an intimate, personal relationship with God, it has become a wall that isolates us from God. Jesus said this to those people who had replaced God with the scripture: *"You diligently study the Scriptures because you think that by them you possess eternal life. These are the Scriptures that testify about me, yet you refuse to come to me to have life"* (John 5:39–40 NIV).

Life is not found in a scripture. Life is not found in a doctrine or idea. Life is found in Jesus. It is through intimate, personal involvement with Him that we partake of who He is and what He has to offer. The life is in the Son! He who has the Son has life.[1] We have tried to put life in the Bible. We have tried to put life in prayer. We have tried to put life in worship. All those things facilitate life. They are part of our relationship with the One who possesses life. But none of these activities are a substitute for Jesus, the One who has the life and shares the life.

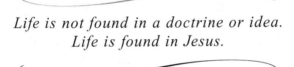

Life is not found in a doctrine or idea.
Life is found in Jesus.

None of those activities have life, and none of those activities can make us righteous. They do not have the power of righteousness. The power of righteousness abides in Him and Him alone. As I commune with Him and connect to the reality that I am in Him, I connect with His righteousness. I only experience the power of righteousness to the degree that I connect to Jesus personally.

When He is my source of life, power, peace, and righteousness, I can discover I am wrong about a doctrine and not feel threatened. I can admit to personal failure and not be afraid. I can discover my sin and never feel ashamed.

This is radical righteousness! And this is better than anything that fits into the logic of man! After all, God did say, *"No eye has seen, no ear has heard, no mind has conceived what God has prepared for those who love him"* (1 Corinthians 2:9 NIV). We are

---

1.   See 1 John 5:12.

*I only experience the power of righteousness
to the degree that I connect to Jesus personally.*

so out of touch with the goodness of God that we cannot conceive of the idea that He would come up with a better Gospel than the one we have created in our limited mind.

Do You Want Reasonable or Radical?

We so need to be in charge that we want to dictate God's righteousness. We want Him to come up with a plan that makes sense to us. It must fit into our carnal logic. We want a reasonable righteousness, but God is offering a radical righteousness. He is offering something that can so alter our sense of self that we detach ourselves from all feelings of lack and inadequacies. He has something so radical it can overcome every failure, every fear, every aspect of lack. It can break us out of the cycle and destruction. It can launch us into the fulfillment of every promise God ever made….to anyone!

*We want a reasonable righteousness,
but God is offering a radical righteousness.*

Is it possible that our issues about righteousness revolve around our fear that someone less deserving than us might receive more than they deserve? These types of feelings are especially prevalent when we see someone who isn't as "qualified" as us, but they seem to live a better life. They seem to be more in touch with God. They even seem to be getting more of the promises and blessings. This is so unfair!

It only seems unfair because we have rejected the righteousness of God. It seems that we are propelled into works righteousness more when we compare ourselves to others than any other time. If a person less deserving than me receives more of the benefits of the New Covenant than I do, then I am confronted with my issues of unbelief. Even though I am more deserving, I have to admit that I do not trust the righteousness of God as much as that other person. I am forced to face my self-imposed limitations and my self-righteous, condescending attitude.

Like Job, we would rather condemn God in an attempt to preserve our own righteousness than to face the real issues. God asked Job, *"Would you discredit my justice? Would you condemn me to justify yourself?"* (Job 40:8 NIV). The answer to that is an overwhelming YES! Yes, I will create a doctrine to explain why I am not receiving from God. Living in this pain is better than admitting to being wrong.

Face it, this Gospel is unfair and illogical! But it works, and no substitute has ever had the power of this Gospel. In describing this unfair, unreasonable Gospel, Paul said, *"Blessed are those whose lawless deeds are forgiven, and whose sins are covered; blessed is the man to whom the Lord shall not impute sin"* (Romans 4:7–8).

*This Gospel is unfair
and illogical! But it works.*

A person who is blessed is someone who is fortunate and to be envied. This incredible favor of God is available to all mankind through the finished work of Jesus. We have the opportunity to stand before God in His righteousness—a righteousness we did not earn and a favor we do not deserve. The world should be so envious of the favor, the joy, the peace, and the abundance that we experience that they would be driven to know this same God and experience this same blessing.

Instead, the church is envying one another. Our unbelief of the righteousness of God in Jesus alienates us from these incredible blessings and we become angry at those who receive them. In fact, we get so angry that we fuss and argue. We complain and slander. We live in lack and despise those who are getting better than they deserve. Instead of rejoicing at the goodness of God and being encouraged to accept it as our own, we fight against it. We will not enter in, and we prevent others from entering in.

Paul said that the only way we could see what was beyond the scope of our human comprehension was by the Holy Spirit: *"but God has revealed it to us by his Spirit"* (1 Corinthians 2:10 NIV). All that we cannot see with our intellect God can show us by His Spirit. If you want to continue to live in mediocre results, just continue to embrace a mediocre gospel. But if you want radial results, give yourself fully to the righteousness of Jesus and allow the Holy Spirit to take you to a place beyond your wildest imagination!

Jesus lived a radical life and faced a radical death to give us radical promises. He met every requirement so every promise would be sure and absolute. Go ahead! Live a radical life of love and peace that passes all comprehension. Trust Jesus for what you cannot do and to fully qualify you for all God's promises.

CHAPTER 19

THE REALITIES OF RIGHTEOUSNESS

"Jim, is there something wrong with me?" Sherry asked. "I feel like such a dunce! Why am I having trouble getting this?"

"People have struggled with this since the resurrection of Jesus," I assured her. "Don't be too hard on yourself."

Her excitement seemed to be growing and her eyes sparkled as our discussion continued. "It's like I get a piece of this and then suddenly it's bigger than I can grasp again," she explained.

"That's exactly how it is," I replied. "The realities of righteousness are always more than anyone can completely grasp. No matter what you see, you suddenly realize there's more! Life in the spirit is a never-ending adventure into the realities of righteousness."

The righteousness of Jesus is such an incredible reality that we will never get it down to an intellectual definition that satisfies our mind. What's more important than finding a complete definition is that it become an experiential reality that guides and empowers our life. We need to feel righteousness more than we need to define righteousness. We must allow the sense of righteousness and completeness to overtake the sense of lack.

When Paul wrote to the Romans, he explained that faith righteousness was the stumbling stone of the Gospel. It is the point that presents the greatest struggle for the greatest number of people. *"For they stumbled at that stumbling stone. As it is written: 'Behold, I lay in Zion a stumbling stone and rock of offense, and whoever believes on Him will not be put to shame' "* (Romans 9:32–33). Our choices are simple. We can stumble over this rock of offense or we can stand on it and be secure. We can fall on it and be broken, or it can fall on us and we can be crushed.[1] We can argue over definitions of it or we can yield ourselves to its power.

The realities of righteousness will never be grasped by those seeking theoretical understanding. The power of righteousness is grasped by those who put it into practice as a way of life. Hebrews 5:13–14 says it like this: *"Anyone who lives on milk, being still an infant, is not acquainted with the teaching about righteousness. But solid food is for the mature, who by constant use have trained themselves to distinguish good from evil"* (NIV). Those

The power of righteousness is grasped
by those who put it into practice as a way of life.

who commit to live in the righteousness of Jesus have an experience that supercedes any argument. Experience allows one to grasp what he cannot fully explain!

Resurrection Power

When Jesus was crucified, He became our sin. He became our sin so we would not have to live in sin. He took all the curse of the law. He took the punishment we would have deserved. He was chastened by God so we would not fear God's punishing us. When Jesus cried out, "Father, why have You forsaken Me," He was experiencing what we would have experienced had we died in our sin. He was separated from God

---

1.   See Luke 20:18.

so we would never be separated from God. He died a sinner's death so we would never have to die. Our sins put Him in the grave.

We know that after Jesus was crucified, He obtained righteousness by faith. Paul said that he didn't want to be found in a righteousness of his own. He wanted the righteousness that came by the faith of Jesus. You see, Jesus had to overcome our sin by His faith. He trusted God to raise Him up in righteousness. It is that righteousness that is at work in us. Paul went on to say, *"And be found in him, not having mine own righteousness, which is of the law, but that which is through the faith of Christ, the righteousness which is of God by faith"* (Philippians 3:9 KJV).

It is that very power, the resurrection power, the power in the righteousness of God, that exploded in Jesus and raised Him from the death of sin. It is by this power that He took the keys of death and hell. It is by this power that He conquered every principality, every power, and every name that is named. And it is this power that is at work in us who believe— this same power that raised Jesus from the dead. Paul prayed that we would get a revelation of this so our lives would be empowered by the resurrection power of Jesus.[2]

When we believed on Jesus, we believed that God raised Him from the dead. The secret power of the kingdom of God, however, is found in what we believe about the resurrection of Jesus. When I am faced with sin, the wrong question to ask is, "Do I have enough faith to overcome this?" The key questions should be these: "Did Jesus overcome this when He was raised from the dead? Am I in Him?" If so, then I get to share in His inheritance. When faced with poverty, I have to ask, "Did Jesus overcome poverty when He was raised from the dead? Am I in Him?" Then I too have overcome poverty. When faced with sickness, I have to ask, "Did Jesus overcome sickness

---

2.   Read Ephesians 1:17–23.

when He was raised from the dead? Am I in Him?" Then I too have overcome sickness. Why? It is because the same power that was at work in Him is at work in me right now.

The key questions should be these: "Did Jesus overcome this when He was raised from the dead? Am I in Him?"

If the resurrection power did not fail Jesus, then it cannot fail me. When we link our faith and our hope to the resurrection of Jesus, we can't help but win. His resurrection gave us evidence. When we need anything that God has we have to ask, "Did Jesus receive this as part of His inheritance? Am I in Him?" Then it is ours as well. This is what the scripture means when it says we are *"joint heirs with Christ"* (Romans 8:17). If He has it, it is ours. We share in all He obtains. He can't leave us out of His inheritance. So if He is righteous, then we are righteous because we are in Him.

To rise above lack and break out of our repetitive cycle of ups and downs, we need to see Jesus as He is today, seated at the right hand of God and filled with righteousness. Then we need to see ourselves in Him, sharing in all His inheritance, rejoicing in what He received by His faith!

This is the secret of walking in the Spirit. Our current paradigm of spirituality stirs images of someone walking about in an esoteric state with his eyes glazed over. Although there is nothing wrong with experiencing euphoria in the presence of God, that is not necessarily what the New Testament refers to when it talks about life in the Spirit.

The Secret to Living in the Spirit

Life in the Spirit is juxtaposed against life in the flesh. One connects you with the power of the Holy Spirit. The other connects you to the power of your flesh, to your own natural abilities. Paul said, *"The righteous requirement of the law might be fulfilled in us who do not walk according to the flesh but according to the Spirit"* (Romans 8:4). So, if I can "walk in the spirit," I not only will possess righteousness, but I also will live righteous.

Let's look at it this way. My body (flesh) has five senses. These senses put me in touch with the natural world. By those senses I know, experience, and function in the natural world. I also have a spirit, and in my spirit I have the same five senses. Those senses put me in touch with God. Those who are in the flesh seek to experience God through their five natural senses. They want something to happen in this natural realm to make them feel righteous.

When people experience life in the Spirit, they do not look to the natural to understand and experience God. Instead, they look to what Jesus has done in their spirit. They are not seeking empowerment in their natural man; rather, they expect the power of the Holy Spirit in them to give them strength. They are renewing their mind based on what has happened in their spirit. The person in the flesh, on the other hand, judges the effectiveness of God by what he experiences in his natural senses. Such people are carnal minded.

Paul so eloquently explained their plight.

For those who live according to the flesh set their minds on the things of the flesh, but those who live according to the Spirit, the things of the Spirit. For to be carnally minded is death, but to be spiritually minded is life and peace. Because the carnal mind is enmity against God; for it is not subject to the law of God, nor indeed can be. So then, those who are in the flesh cannot please God. But you are not in the flesh but in the Spirit, if indeed the Spirit of God dwells in you. Now if anyone does not have the Spirit of Christ, he is not His (Romans 8:5–9).

The person who wants to experience God through his natural senses does not and will not understand. The realities of righteousness can never be comprehended or experienced through the natural senses. Thus, the carnal man has limited his experience with God to the finite world of the five senses and his limited comprehension.

How about you? Where are you looking to experience God? Are you looking to the finished reality that your spirit has been made perfect, is righteous, and lacks nothing? Are you seeking to experience what the Holy Spirit has already done in you? Or are you looking for what will happen in your outer man? Are you looking for some future experience or a

The realities of righteousness can never be comprehended or experienced through the natural senses.

past reality? In other words, is your righteousness a past tense reality or a future hope?

Fill yourself with the knowledge of all that God has done in your inner man. Renew your mind so that all you see of yourself is based on what Jesus has done in you. As the internal reality becomes your conscious reality, you will experience a flow in the power of God beyond your wildest dreams. This is unlike the sensations based on the five senses that come and go with the passing of time. They connect you to lack and drive you to seek a new experience to validate you standing with God. Rather, because God abides in your inner man, you will have an abiding sense of God and His righteousness. Just as my friend Sherry discovered, there will never be an end to your new discoveries in the realities of God's righteousness. Every day can be a new adventure in righteousness!

CHAPTER 20

SETTING THE THERMOSTAT

God has always desired that mankind live in wholeness. He never intended for us to experience lack on any level. God has always worked to give us the very best, despite our endless attempts at thwarting the plan.

In the beginning God put mankind in paradise. There was no sickness, poverty, pain, or suffering there. If those things had been God's will, they would have been present at the beginning. Adam, as the first man, never experienced lack until he doubted God's promise and began to act independent of God's plan.

When God restores all things to Himself, mankind will once again enter that state of complete wholeness. When heaven is established on planet Earth there will be no sickness, sorrow, death, or pain. We will not lack in any manner. We will finally be restored to the standard of living for which we were created.

Mankind cannot function normally in a state of lack. We do not possess the emotional capacity for it. In the beginning we were crowned with glory and honor,[1] without which our sense of self is incomplete. Man has to feel right about himself and about his relationship to God or he enters an emotional realm beyond his capacity to function.

When mankind rebelled against God's wisdom, he brought sin, fear, death, and lack to every level of his existence. He had

---

1.   See Hebrews 2:5–8.

the emotional need for wholeness, dignity, and worth, yet, he had severed himself from the only source where those could be obtained. Thus, for six thousand years man has vainly attempted to recover a proper sense of self apart from God. It won't happen! In fact, the more we do to find that sense of dignity and worth on our own, the worse the problem becomes.

In Jesus, God created a way for us to recover our sense of dignity and worth, to be qualified for all His promises, and to live as God intended—as nearly as possible in this world. God's incredible love drove Him to devise a plan that would make wholeness possible in a world corrupted by sin. He would give mankind an incorruptible nature. People would once again be able to approach God without fear. We would be eligible for all the promises. And, finally, we could feel right about ourselves and God.

One Sure Covenant

It was essential to God that His children once again have sure access to all His provision. At the same time, He knew that mankind would never have the ability to achieve the level of righteousness required to receive the promises. So, instead of making a covenant with each individual on the planet, God made a covenant with Jesus. In Galatians 3:16 Paul explained this subtle but essential twist in God's plan. *"Now to Abraham and his Seed were the promises made. He does not say, 'And to seeds,' as of many, but as of one, 'And to your Seed,' who is Christ."*

Instead of making a covenant with each individual on the planet, God made a covenant with Jesus.

God did not make a covenant with a group of individuals. If His covenant was with us as individuals, we would be responsible to live up to every part of the law in order to receive the inheritance. None of us could ever do it. If the covenant was with us as individuals, then the moment we failed at any one point the covenant would be annulled and could never be restored. The promises would not be sure to all.

God made this covenant where it could not be changed or annulled. *"Brethren, I speak in the manner of men: Though it is only a man's covenant, yet if it is confirmed, no one annuls or adds to it"* (Galatians 3:15). It was essential that this covenant be unchangeable in order to make it sure for all people.

The writer of the book of Hebrews explained the covenant that God made in terms of a last will and testament. He explained that once the testator of a will dies, that will goes into force and cannot be changed. In Hebrews 9:15 (NIV) he explained this in terms we can understand. *"For this reason Christ is the mediator of a new covenant, that those who are called may receive the promised eternal inheritance—now that he has died."* Above all else, God wanted to make sure eternal life was absolute for all mankind.

In verses 16 and 17 (NIV) he continued to explain, *"In the case of a will, it is necessary to prove the death of the one who made it, because a will is in force only when somebody has died; it never*

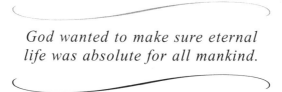

God wanted to make sure eternal life was absolute for all mankind.

takes effect while the one who made it is living." When Jesus died, this last will and testament went into effect. It could not be changed. He fulfilled all the righteous requirements of the law. He did what we cannot do. By His faith and obedience He obtained a more excellent covenant than the first covenant. Now that He has died, it can't be broken, changed, or modified.

Unlike other covenants or wills where the testator dies and the will can be contested by the survivors, Jesus was raised up in righteousness and lives forever to enforce the covenant He established by His own blood. This covenant is sure! He has risen to enforce every promise.

Jesus' faith obtained the covenant. All we have to do is believe that God raised Jesus from the dead and follow Him as Lord. Then we are in Him, and we live in Him by faith. As Paul said in Acts 17:28, *"For in him we live, and move, and have our being"* (KJV). Because of all He has done, I can trust Him as Lord. I can give Him my whole heart! Because I am in Him, all He has is mine. He is the heir, but I am the joint heir.[2] Because I abide in Him, I have access to all He possesses.

I can't break this covenant. I can't mess this up. If I choose not to follow Jesus as Lord, I may put myself in a place where I cannot receive what He has, but I don't lose legal right to the inheritance. The moment I turn my heart to Him, I align myself once again with His flow of blessings. It is only at these times of personal failure that I question the assurance of His covenant.

We all will face failure in our personal lives. But God, in His incredible love and wisdom, made sure that His provisions would always be available for us. He created this realm of living called the kingdom of God. We may interrupt the flow of His incredible goodness, but we cannot annul the covenant. It belongs to Jesus, not to us.

We cannot annul the covenant.
It belongs to Jesus, not to us.

Where Is Your Heart Set?

The carnal-minded person, the individual who has his mind set on the flesh, interprets all that he sees and experiences

---

2.   See Romans 8:17.

in light of the five senses. He assumes that the outside is the measure of the inside. When his outward man deviates, the carnal mind says, "You are not righteous." His heart then condemns him and he loses confidence. That is why, if you allow your mind to follow the logic (*logos*) of the flesh, you will never find your way out of failure. Your judgments will bind you to a life of pain and failure. Your sense of reality will be distorted, and your concepts of God will be limited.

Failure is an unfortunate reality of life. All people will at some time face an ethical or moral failure. The question is not, "Will I ever fail?" The question is, "How will I respond?" If you begin to judge your spiritual life by the failures of the flesh, you will talk yourself into an abyss of desperate emotions.

Proverbs 24:16 says, *"A righteous man may fall seven times and rise again."* Personal failure does not prove that you are not righteous. When the righteous fall, their new nature compels

The question is not, "Will I ever fail?"
The question is, "How will I respond?"

them to get up again and again. The just can't stay down. So having a new nature does not mean you never fall. It means it is not natural for you to accept failure as the end. The fact that you keep getting up proves that you have a righteous nature.

People who are connected to a sense of righteousness through Jesus cannot stay down. They have trained themselves to pay attention to the inner voice, to the witness of the Holy Spirit, reminding them that they are in Jesus. They yield to the voice of their heart as it proclaims their righteousness.

When we were born again, we obtained a righteous nature. Our spirit came alive to God because He took up residence in us. Having a new nature means there is a new influence in our life. But we have to let that new influence work. If we renew our mind and establish our heart in our new identity, then we experience the power to live in that identity. If we do not renew our mind, then we have this internal struggle between our spirit and our mind. In the end the conflict of these two voices shape the beliefs of the heart.

The person who is connected to lack expects to fall. He has no confidence in the power of righteousness that is at work in him. When he fails, the ensuing condemnation is simply a false confirmation of what he believed about himself all along. He is trapped in a cycle of defeat.

Even when his life rises to higher standards of godliness, he still expects the fall. The person connected to lack starts to worry when too many things go right. His heart tells him that he is living at a place that can't possibly last. It is too good to be true.

The heart is much like a thermostat. A thermostat does not kick in every time the temperature vacillates a single degree. No, the temperature may rise or fall several degrees before the thermostat kicks in. Your behavior may fall below your normal standard of ethics and morality, but your behavior is not at every moment indicative of the condition of your spirit.

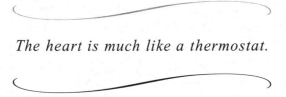

The heart is much like a thermostat.

When your behavior sinks to a certain level, it is as if your heart says, "Oh no! This is not who we are; we've got to do something about this." If we believe we are righteous, our heart will allow the righteousness of God that lives in us to empower us to rise above that sin.

The problem comes when we have not established our heart in faith righteousness. If we do not believe we are righteous, if we have a heart that is corrupted by religion or unbelief, then it never allows a release of righteousness. We never experience the righteous power of God that flows through us and gives us absolute victory. It's like our heater works, but our faulty thermostat keeps it from kicking on and warming the house.

As a matter of fact, the person who has not established his heart in faith righteousness has just the opposite experience. His heart acts as a thermostat to pull him back down to the level of his perceived righteousness.

Any feeling, any thought, anything that makes you believe you are not righteous, is a lie. Your problem is not a lack of righteousness. Your problem is you need to reset the thermostat.

Meditating on the Word is one way to connect to the righteousness of God. Spend time pondering the hundreds of scriptures that talk about your new identity in Jesus. Discover

Your problem is not a lack of righteousness.
Your problem is you need to reset the thermostat.

God's view of you and make it your own. Refuse to see yourself as anything other than righteous. Persuading your heart is like resetting the thermostat. The level you set your thermostat is the level at which you live. Start to reset your heart today. The setting of your thermostat is your choice. You are the one who convinces your heart that this is who you are in Jesus. The Spirit of God in you will then provide the power to change the spiritual temperature!

Chapter 21

Getting It in Your Heart

"I know Jesus died for me," came the sarcastic complaint. "But it hasn't done all that much for my life! I don't know where you get all this stuff, anyway." Like so many people, Terence thought that having the information should be enough. He had an intellectual concept of God, but his life had changed very little. Rather than take personal responsibility for his situation, he found it more convenient to blame God.

"The Bible didn't say that if you had the information about the truth it would change your life. It said you had to believe it in your heart," I reasoned.

"Believe in your heart!" he fired back. "I don't know what you're talking about. All this heart stuff is just religious double talk," came the pseudo-intellectual argument.

Terence thought that a bachelor's degree in psychology elevated him above the realm of what he considered to be religious superstition. Like too many people, his biased views didn't allow room for the oldest proven science book in the world—the Bible. (And to add insult to injury, he wasn't even on top of the latest "cutting edge" discoveries in medicine or psychology.) He simply thought that winning the argument was equal to experiencing victory.

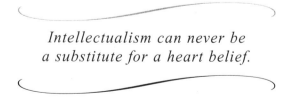

Intellectualism can never be
a substitute for a heart belief.

The Bible never even hints that intellectual consent will change your life. Information alone does not empower anyone to change. Jesus said that truth must be believed in the heart and put into practice. Then and only then does it have the power to set you free. Intellectualism can never be a substitute for a heart belief.

The Heart Makes the Difference

The heart factor seems to be one of the key elements we leave out of our walk with God. Until recently, we thought the heart was some metaphoric terminology that didn't need to be understood or explored. However, as we come to understand more about the complexities of the human psyche and the mind-body connection, we realize that there is more to the heart than we ever thought possible.

In his book *The Heart's Code*, Dr. Paul Pearsall points out that the heart has more neurons than the brain. In other words, the heart has the capacity for memory. Oriental science and medicine has long understood that the heart facilitates long-term memory. It is this long-term memory of the heart that gives us our knowledge of self. We are the sum total of our life's experiences; it is the memory of those experiences that gives us our sense of self.

When the Bible talks about believing in the heart, we must realize that any belief of the heart will affect our sense of self. In other words, when we believe a truth from the Word of God, it will change the way we see ourselves. Until it does, it is not believed at the heart level. It is simply a bit of mental, intellectual information.

Our view of the world is determined by how we see ourselves. When we alter our view of ourselves, we see the world differently. Our heart is the filter through which we interpret our world. A heart filled with lack, inadequacy, or low self-worth interprets the world in a way that keeps a person bound in these negative strengths. Our self-perception molds the chain that imprisons us.

When we believe the Word of God in our heart, it not only changes how we see ourselves, but it also changes how we see ourselves in every situation. For example, if you feel like a failure, you will interpret your world as a hard and difficult place

*Any belief of the heart
will affect our sense of self.*

with no opportunity. Thus you will create the world you perceive by your choices. If you feel desperate, your next relationship decision will be made like a desperate person would make it. If you feel financially limited, you will make your next financial decision based on the mind-set of a person in poverty. Although you may make an occasional right choice, the overall direction of your life will not be what you really want. As the saying goes, even a blind squirrel finds a nut every now and then. These occasional blunders into fulfillment justify a continuance of our present paradigm.

On the other hand, when you feel righteous, you consistently make decisions like a righteous person would make. When you feel successful, you see the world as a place of opportunity. Your heart leads you to make decisions that create the world you live in. Then it empowers you to live in that world.

*Your heart leads you to make
decisions that create the world you live in.*

Romans 10:9–10 promises, *"If you confess with your mouth the Lord Jesus and believe in your heart that God has raised Him from the dead, you will be saved. For with the heart one believes unto righteousness, and with the mouth confession is made unto salvation."* This is God's prescription for experiencing salvation.

Salvation Is…

Salvation (*sozo*) is usually understood to be only the born-again experience. However, to the man on the street in New Testament times, it meant healed, saved, delivered, blessed, prospered, protected, set apart, and made whole. In other words, any aspect of the abundant life that God offers is experienced to the degree that we believe the truth about Jesus' resurrection in our heart and acknowledge it with our mouth.

At best we often hold only a historic concept of the resurrection. We believe that He died and rose from the dead. Evidently, however, there is something more I should believe about the resurrection that will change the way I see myself.

If I believe that I am in Jesus, then His every victory at the resurrection becomes my victory. If I believe in my heart that Jesus was raised from the dead, conquering sickness, it will change how I see myself as susceptible to sickness. If I believe, in my heart, that Jesus conquered poverty through His resurrection, it will change how I see myself in relation to poverty. Whatever I believe about Jesus' victory at the resurrection becomes my personal victory when I believe it in my heart. Anything you believe in your heart always changes the way you see yourself!

Living in wholeness through the righteous power of God happens when I believe in my heart that God raised Jesus from the dead and I acknowledge Him as Lord. In other words, I commit to following Him fully.

Take the Next Step

The question is, what am I prepared to do to bring myself to the place where I believe this truth in my heart? There are several tools that I can use to write it on my heart. One of the most effective is meditation. Meditation is the key to changing beliefs of the heart. So how do I implement the exhortation to meditate on the Word of God? Keep in mind that meditation is a heart exercise. I want to meditate on the Word in a way that influences my heart. Therefore, I should take a particular promise from God's Word and ponder it in a way that I see myself living it. Until I can see it changing my life, I am not affecting my heart. As I see myself living and experiencing that promise, I need to allow myself to experience what it feels like to have it working in my life.

Let me give you an example. After several operations and years of sickness, I lay in bed completely discouraged. I was too weak to pray. I could only lift my arms for a few minutes at a time. As I lay in bed on the verge of giving up, I was reminded of the power of meditating on God's Word. So I closed my eyes and pictured myself out of the hospital, playing with my children, and doing the things that I would do if I were actually well. I thought about it and saw those images until I felt the joy of the experience. It felt real.

Meditation is actually a combination of information and emotion. God gave us a right- and left-sided brain. Studies show that when we combine both sides of our brain in any effort we can learn more quickly with a more lasting effect. When I combine information and emotion, I begin to experience my thoughts as real. Appropriately, someone once said that the heart knows no difference between reality and something clearly imagined. When I experience a thought at an emotional level, it heightens my ability to believe that it is real. It is a way of connecting with a reality different than what I am experiencing.

Like the apostle Paul, who learned the secret power of seeing the unseen, we can see our future through the eyes of the heart. As we see ourselves experiencing God's promises to the degree that we begin to create the sense of actually possessing those promises, they become our reality. Once it becomes believable, the heart will release the power of God to make it happen.

When I combine information and emotion,
I begin to experience my thoughts as real.

Whether we are confessing the Word, praying, or worshiping—all of which are tools for transformation—we should always see ourselves experiencing the end result of God's promise. We should see and experience that promise as real until it becomes the reality of our heart. After months of meditating on the Word of God, health and healing became more real to me than sickness. To the degree that I could see it in my heart, sickness lost its grip on my life and I was overtaken with health and healing.

Turn every interaction with God into a meditative experience. Whether you are praying, confessing, or worshiping, involve your heart. Take yourself to that place where you see yourself experiencing every word you sing, say, or pray. Get the Word into your heart and change your reality forever!

Any part of life where you are not experiencing the reality of God can be changed. Find a scripture that promises you a different and better quality of life. Memorize that scripture. Then personalize it. Put it in the first person. For example, you may use the scripture that says, *"And you shall remember the Lord your God, for it is He who gives you power to get wealth"* (Deuteronomy 8:18).

It could be personalized like this: "I always remember You, Lord God, and I thank You that You have given me the power to get wealth. Every day I am seeing and seizing new opportunities. I am diligent, faithful, and hardworking. I am prospering beyond my personal capacity. I am experiencing Your capacity for wealth!"

As you ponder this verse, imagine what it would look like if that was real today. How would you live? Where would you live? How would it change your life? What levels of new happiness and contentment would it bring? See all of these benefits. Ponder them until you experience the joy. Then simply acknowledge, "I thank You that this is my reality, based on Your promise. By Your grace this is mine now, and I will walk into it day by day."

Every time you consider your financial situation, this would be your meditation. Do it first thing in the morning and last thing at night. When this becomes more real to you than the power of your current life, it will overtake you and become your present reality. Do this regarding righteousness. Do this about peace. Do this for every area of your life. If you need help, use *The Prayer Organizer*[1] and write the Word of God on every corner of your heart for every area of God's promises!

---

1. You can obtain *The Prayer Organizer* by contacting Impact International Publications, 3516 S. Broad Place, Huntsville, AL, 35805, or by logging on to www.impactministries.com.

CHAPTER 22

BREAKING THE CYCLE

F reedom from the cycle begins where the sense of lack ends. Do you want to live the abundant life? Then you must experience fullness in Jesus. Paul said it like this: *"And I pray that you, being rooted and established in love, may have power, together with all the saints, to grasp how wide and long and high and deep is the love of Christ, and to know this love that surpasses knowledge— that you may be filled to the measure of all the fullness of God"* (Ephesians 3:17–19 NIV).

Because Adam didn't grasp the love of God, he surrendered his wholeness on the assumption that God had not given him the best. He didn't believe he was who God said he was. Therefore, it was impossible for him to believe he could receive the best life had to offer. As a result, he declared his independence and sought to establish his identity by his own means.

Ancient Israel also is a model of mankind continuing to doubt God's acceptance as a special people. They repeatedly put God to the test. They refused to believe that He could and would in fact fulfill all His promises. They died in the wilderness because they did not believe God's promises to them. They could not find that place of rest, the point at which they ceased from their own labors. Instead, they rejected God and sought to qualify for the promises on their own merit.

The sin nature has one essential flaw: fear. From the emotional base of fear emerges every other negative emotion and every aspect of unbelief. Fear does not believe that God is a good God. Fear makes the idea of the unconditional love of God seem irrational and illogical. Thus, the degree that we are motivated by fear, is the degree we are dominated by the mind-set of lack. Fear is the emotional perspective that grows out of our sin nature. On the other hand, the degree that we accept righteousness as a free gift is the degree that we will believe we are eligible for God's unconditional love. And the more we are immersed in the love of God, the more our faith abounds. As our faith explodes beyond the limits of our carnal logic, we experience the fullness of God.

Jesus Overcame Satan's Strategy

When Satan came to Jesus in Matthew 4, he used the same strategy he had used on Adam. And why not? It had worked successfully for four thousand years. Man had consistently questioned his relationship to God. We have adamantly refused to believe that we are who God says we are. Therefore, we cannot conceive that God would do what He said He would do. We reject the promise and seek the kingdom through works. And the more we doubt our identity, the more we are plunged into lack and dead works.

Jesus, the second Adam, withstood the deception. Satan's attempt to lure Him into proving His identity by His performance was intended to start Jesus down the pathway to lack. He intended for Jesus to reach the same conclusion that Adam had reached four thousand years earlier: "I am not who God says I am." For Jesus to have worked a single miracle to prove He was the Son of God, He first would have had to doubt that He was who God said He was. But there was no need to prove that which was believed! His trust in His identity kept Him connected to the sense of fullness. He had no sense of lack even though He was tired and hungry.

This battle over His identity was one Jesus fought all the way through His earthly ministry, to the crucifixion, to the resurrection and the throne. It was this one belief that empowered Him to start His earthly ministry, work miracles, be raised from the dead, conquer Satan, and fulfill all the requirements to establish the New Covenant. Had He lost His sense of identity, He would have lost the battle. He would never have been raised from the dead! We all would have been doomed to an eternity without God!

Paul said, *"Christ was raised from the dead by the glory of the Father"* (Romans 6:4). The greatness, the glory, the brilliance of God is made real because it is God's view, God's opinion. It is His reality! Like each of us, Jesus had to choose His own reality. He could take what the circumstances dictated or He could choose what God said in His Word.

As Jesus hung on the cross, the one consistent accusation He heard was, "If You are the Son of God, take yourself down from this cross." His sense of identity never wavered, even in the face of incredibly contradictory circumstances. He refused to accept that as the final reality.

Even in the grave He clung to His identity. He acknowledged that He was a priest forever after the order of Melchizedek. He acknowledged that His soul would not be left in hell, neither would His body see corruption. He acknowledged that all His enemies would become His footstool. He acknowledged everything that God said about Him, until that became such a powerful reality that it changed the circumstance. When His identity became His reality, He was raised from the dead.[1] When your identity in Jesus becomes your reality, your circumstances will no longer be able to hold you.

Just as He had done on the mount of temptation and throughout His earthly ministry, He stayed focused on who

---

1.   See Hebrews 5:6; 6:20; 7:17,21; Acts 2:31; Psalm 16:10; Hebrews 10:13.

He was in relation to God. Although all His circumstances denied God's reality, He never accepted those circumstances as His reality. He acknowledged God's view and opinion, and He experienced it as His reality. He experienced resurrection power because He knew who He was.

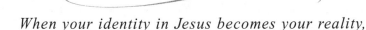

When your identity in Jesus becomes your reality, your circumstances will no longer be able to hold you.

It is the same for us. We live life out of who we are, not out of what we can do. What we can do and should do emerges freely from our sense of self. It is our identity in Jesus, the absolute assurance that we are who God says we are, that empowers us to live this incredible life of abundance. Without the menacing, undermining sensations of lack, the world looks like a different place. As we leave lack behind, a whole new world begins to emerge—a world of opportunity and promise. Like Hagar who was abandoned in the desert and saw no hope of survival, our eyes can be opened to a world of incredible provision and limitless resources.[2] The land of lack starts to look like the land of opportunity!

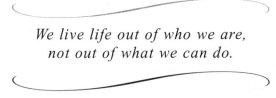

We live life out of who we are, not out of what we can do.

We all must renew our mind to see God's realities as our own, or else we will be trapped in the world of illusion created by the mind of unbelief. God did not dig a well for Hagar. Instead, He opened her eyes to see what was there all the time.

---

2.   See Genesis 21:14–20.

The sense of desperation and lack blinded her to the resources that were available. With just a slight change in perception, she was added to that list of people who lived in a realm that could only be accessed by faith and empowered by grace. Like Moses, Paul, and all those in the roll call of faith in Hebrews 11, she escaped the visible by seeing the invisible.

Learning Paul's Secret to Abundant Life

The apostle Paul was sustained by a reality that no one could see or conceive as he pioneered the message of faith righteousness to a hostile religious world. In 2 Corinthians 4:16–17 he said, *"Therefore we do not lose heart. Even though our outward man is perishing, yet the inward man is being renewed day by day. For our light affliction, which is but for a moment, is working for us a far more exceeding and eternal weight of glory."* My mind staggers as I read this phrase, *"our light affliction."* His sense of reality was certainly not determined by his circumstances.

What did Paul deal with? His life was threatened immediately upon accepting his call; he was rejected by his countrymen; he was not trusted by the church. He was ultimately beaten, stoned to death, shipwrecked, and imprisoned. But none of this seemed to have a great effect on him. It seemed to go almost unnoticed. It is apparent that he was sustained by something more real than what he experienced in this life.

I thank God that Paul didn't stop there without sharing his secret source of supernatural power. In verse 18 he continued, *"While we do not look at the things which are seen, but at the things which are not seen. For the things which are seen are temporary, but the things which are not seen are eternal."* He saw something that could not be seen with the natural eye. He saw God's reality; he saw life from God's perspective. Even with all the tragedy he experienced, this world's system could not drag him back to the lack that drove him when he lived under the law.

Like the Old Testament patriarchs, like Jesus, like Paul and all who have lived by faith, we must choose God's reality in order to escape the confines of this world's system with all its control. As God's opinion replaces our current sense of reality, it begins to give way to the greatness and splendor of God. If you want to live in God's abundance, you must bring

*We must choose God's reality in order
to escape the confines of this world's system.*

all your being, all your emotions, all your intellect, all your senses to believe the truth about your new identity in Jesus. In Him you have a new righteous nature and a new identity!

Lose yourself in God's Word. Die to every sense of self that is not based on the death, burial, and resurrection of Jesus. Look into the perfect law of liberty as a mirror that reflects who you are in Jesus. Like Jesus, who had been bound in the grave by our sin, experience your personal resurrection of righteousness, dignity, and worth.

In 1 Corinthians 13:12 Paul concluded his incredible passage on walking in love with this promise: *"For now we see in a mirror, dimly, but then face to face. Now I know in part, but then I shall know just as I also am known."* He spoke of a time in our life when we grasp the perfect love of God. When we really believe God's love in our heart, we will know ourselves as God knows us. We will see ourselves as God sees us. When we believe God's Word, the image in the mirror changes.

God knows you as holy, sanctified, righteous, loved, accepted, approved, anointed, called, and chosen. What is your perception of yourself? Do you see yourself as God sees you? That will be the revelation that will change your life forever.

Breaking out of the cycle is all about breaking out of your self-perception. Changing how you see yourself is the way you put off the old man and put on the new man. Changing your self-perception is the prerequisite for yielding to righteousness. Change how you see yourself to align with God's view and opinion and you will connect to a wholeness that empowers you to live God's very best. Change how you see yourself and you will discover the power of faith righteousness that takes you from your first prayer, to fulfilling your dreams, to eternity with God. You are who God says you are. Do what it takes to believe that. Do whatever it takes to see yourself as God sees you, and you will break out of the repetitive cycle and leave lack behind.

Breaking out of the cycle is all
about breaking out of your self-perception.

More than twenty years ago, at the lowest point in my life, I was devastated by personal failure, I was incapacitated by a life-threatening disease, and I was drowning in financial debt. I took the Bible and found every scripture about my new identity, I meditated on them, I confessed them, and I prayed and sang them until they became my reality. Today those horrible circumstances seem like a dream. They lost their power over me as I immersed myself in my righteous identity in Jesus. It was from that study that I developed the most powerful tool I have ever created: *The Prayer Organizer*.[3] It became the mirror that reflected my new identity in Jesus.

Now it's time for you to make the change. Die to yourself. Surrender your identity to the cross of Jesus. Lay down the old and pick up the new. Put off the old man and put on the new

---

3.   You can obtain *The Prayer Organizer* by contacting Impact International Publications, 3516 S. Broad Place, Huntsville, AL 35805, or by logging on to www.impactministries.com.

man. Step into this limitless life of peace, power, and all the promises of God!

BREAKING THE CYCLE

THE ULTIMATE SOLUTION TO DESTRUCTIVE PATTERNS

For the free companion video series to this book
and other special offers please visit:

http://www.truepotentialmedia.com/breaking-
the-cycle/